MAKING
Paper Planes

D1370860

*Make and fly your
own paper planes*

MAKING
Paper
Planes

*Make and fly your
own paper planes*

ALEX SCHULTZ

BARNES
& NOBLE
NEW YORK

This edition published by

Barnes & Noble Publishing, Inc.,

by arrangement with Parragon Publishing

2006 Barnes & Noble Books

M 10 9 8 7 6 5 4 3 2 1

ISBN 0-7607-7958-9

Copyright © 2005 by Parragon Books Ltd

All rights reserved. No part of this book may be

used or reproduced, in any manner whatsoever,

without the written permission of the Publisher.

Printed and bound in China

This edition designed by Design Principals

Cover by Talking Design

Text by Alex Schultz

Diagrams by Malcolm Porter

Photography by Roddy Paine

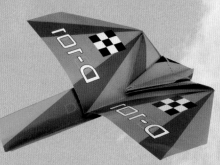

CONTENTS

INTRODUCTION

I first became interested in paper airplanes when my father taught me how to make the Swallow plane which you can find later in this book. The way that paper airplanes glide noiselessly through the air has always fascinated me and I hope it interests you too.

Once you have folded all the planes in this book, you will want to look for the next challenge. You might simply want to compete with your friends. Other people such as Ken Blackburn (world record holder for long-duration flight) decide they want to create a world-beating paper airplane. If this is what you want to do, turn to page 48. There you will find information about the current world records and how you can go about making a record-breaking attempt.

I have been inspired in a different direction. I enjoy developing designs and testing aerodynamic features. I am interested in investigating drag and learning about fluid flow and how it affects real airplanes. The science of fluid dynamics is involved in much of our everyday life. Skyscrapers and bridges are designed to avoid lift adding forces to them which could cause them to fall down. Speedboats, barges and even cruise ships are designed to minimize drag in the water. Swimmers now wear special all-over body suits to decrease drag. Sports cars have specially designed shapes to give them maximum grip by reversing lift, so that they are pushed downwards onto the road.

As a physics student at Cambridge University, England, I am in a brilliant position to learn about all these applications of the science of aerodynamics. Paper airplanes were the inspiration that sparked my interest. Maybe they will do the same for you?

Alex Schultz

At the back of this book (see pages 49-72) we have included patterned pages, which have all the fold lines marked on them, for your first attempt at making the models. Once you have used these, have fun experimenting with different types of paper to make the perfect plane! There are tips on page 10 on choosing paper.

TYPES OF
PAPER PLANES

In this book we look at the three most exciting types of paper airplane: gliders, fighters and weird and wonderful experimental aircraft.

The classic glider is of course a vital ingredient in any book of paper airplanes. It is designed to spend the maximum time in the air and so has a wide wingspan to generate lift. Experiment to find for yourself the best glider in the book. My favorite is the Stealth Bomber. It glides very slowly and silently through the air and does not need a huge amount of initial force to fly well.

The fighters are simply darts. They are created in homage to modern fighter aircraft that have sleek aerodynamic shapes and can fly faster than the speed of sound. Fighter planes like the Draken and the Delta Dart fly best when thrown hard using a fairly flat launch angle. They do not generate much

lift but tend to follow a similar trajectory to a ball or stone being thrown.

The unusual paper airplanes in the Weird and Wonderful section highlight a crucial area of paper airplane design. These planes are groundbreaking and create ideas for new designs and new advances in paper aircraft. Engineers and scientists are often inspired by new ideas which they can never fully understand until they build models of them. This holds true for paper airplane designers too, and some of these designs could be the inspiration for future real aircraft.

Try creating your own paper airplane and then test-fly it. Decide for yourself which category it falls into and also how well it compares with the designs in the book. You could have a world-beater in your hands!

AWZ586

MT-130586

WHY PLANES FLY

Thrust, drag, lift and weight (or gravity) are the four most important forces which act on a plane. The weight of the plane is a force which continually attracts it to the earth. Thrust is created by an engine in a real plane and propels the plane forwards. Paper airplanes get no thrust except when launched and so get their forward propulsion through losing height.

Lift results from the fact that fast-moving air is at lower pressure than slow-moving air. The air above a wing flows faster than the air below the wing and this generates lift. A simple model for the air moving faster over the top of a wing is because it has to travel further to combine again with the flow under the wing, mainly because the top of the wing is more curved. The amount of lift depends on the size and shape of the wing and the speed of the plane.

Drag is easy to imagine. As you stand in the wind or run very fast, you feel a pressure on the front of your body. A plane feels this same pressure as it moves through the air and this is drag. A "stagnation point" occurs where air is stationary at the front of the wing where it divides to flow around it.

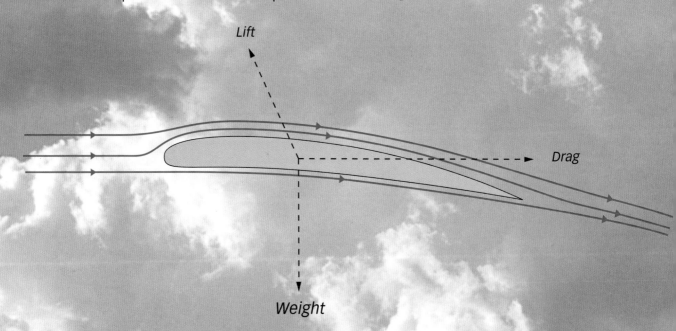

Lift

Drag

Weight

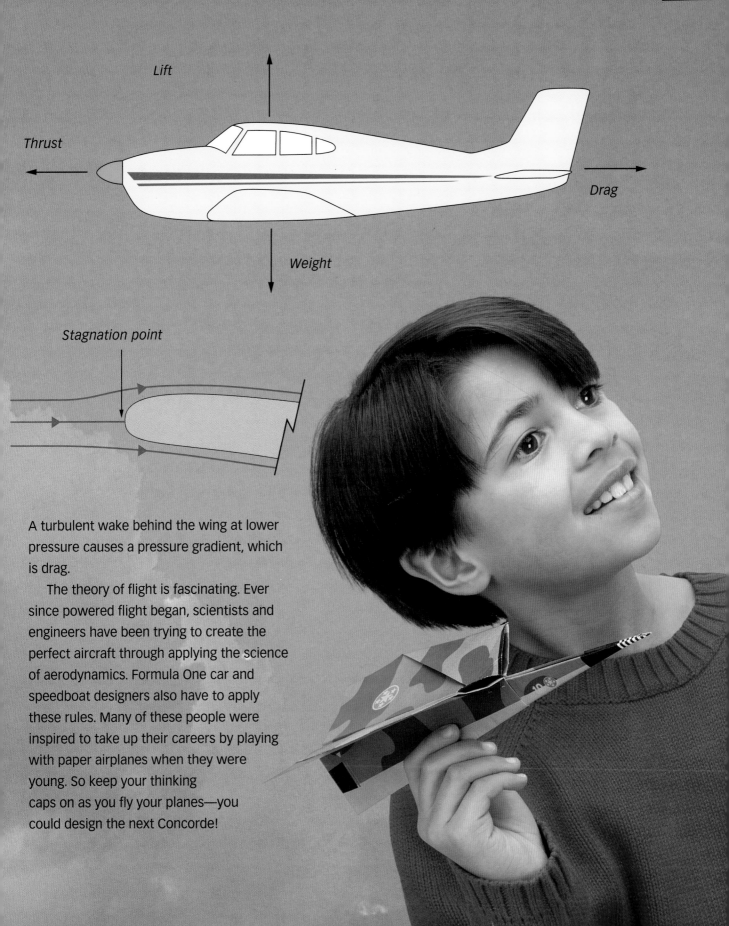

Lift

Thrust

Drag

Weight

Stagnation point

A turbulent wake behind the wing at lower pressure causes a pressure gradient, which is drag.

The theory of flight is fascinating. Ever since powered flight began, scientists and engineers have been trying to create the perfect aircraft through applying the science of aerodynamics. Formula One car and speedboat designers also have to apply these rules. Many of these people were inspired to take up their careers by playing with paper airplanes when they were young. So keep your thinking caps on as you fly your planes—you could design the next Concorde!

GETTING STARTED

Welcome to the fantastic world of paper airplanes. In this section you will learn the basic rules of folding paper and tips on how to makes your planes fly really well. Read it thoroughly and soon your planes will be swooping, gliding and performing aerial stunts with the best of them.

Basic Folds

There are three main basic folds to learn—the valley fold, the mountain fold and the double crease.

The valley fold is made by simply folding one edge of a piece of paper to another. The mountain fold (sometimes called a peak fold) is the reverse of a valley fold in which the paper is folded back on itself.

The third important fold is a double crease. In this fold you first fold along a line as a valley fold, then you unfold this line and fold it again as a mountain fold. It is a very important fold in making paper airplanes because it softens and breaks up the paper along a line allowing it to be more easily manipulated. If you have difficulty with any plane later in this book, such as the Sabertooth or the Swallow perhaps, try replacing some of the folds

with a double crease. This may reduce the lifespan of your planes but it allows you to make more accurate folds.

Tips on Folding

Work on a firm, smooth and clear surface and allow yourself plenty of room to turn your sheet of paper. Score along the crease of the paper with your thumbnail when making a fold. This will ensure a good sharp fold which is vital when making paper airplanes.

Always rotate your paper between folds so that you are in the most comfortable position to make each successive fold. You will probably be most comfortable with the line of the fold nearest to you.

Always make sure that you have aligned your fold correctly before taking the plunge and creasing it. I have ruined so many planes near completion by making the silly mistake of creasing before the fold was accurately aligned.

Types of Paper

There are many types of paper available but not all of them are suitable for making paper airplanes. Officially, for a world record attempt, you must use paper which weighs no more than 100 grams per square metre (100gsm). This means typical photocopier paper, or lighter.

For the gliders in this book lighter types of paper can be better. However, the paper must be rigid enough so that the wings are not floppy when folded. Lightweight, stiff paper makes the best indoor gliders.

For darts, heavier writing paper is better to give you that extra bit of momentum at launch.

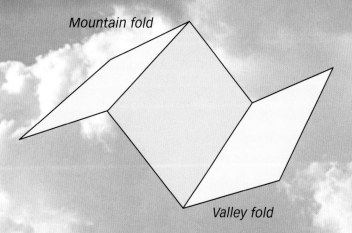

Mountain fold

Valley fold

Making A Square

It is important to be able to make a square quickly and simply from a piece of rectangular paper. The method illustrated here is the best.

Start with an ordinary rectangular sheet of A4 paper.

Take the top left-hand corner and fold it down to lie along the right-hand edge of the sheet. Make sure that the top edge lies exactly along the right-hand edge.

Using the folded-down left-hand edge (which is now parallel to the bottom edge) as a guide, cut carefully along it with scissors. Open out the paper. You now have a perfect square.

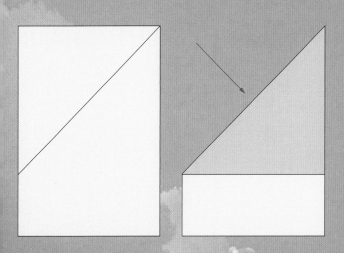

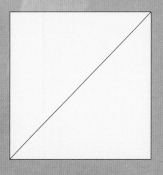

Cutting a perfect square

Flying Tips

To fly your planes successfully, make sure that you follow the instructions provided with each design. Try to ensure that your plane has the same dihedral (the profile of the wings looking down the plane from the nose) as shown in the instructions. Once made, you will need to fine-tune your plane by flight-testing it and this is where much of the real skill lies.

If your plane turns to the left on a test flight, you will need to bend one of the vertical surfaces of your plane to the right or bend up the back of the right-hand wing to compensate for it. These bends act in the same way as the control surfaces of a real plane.

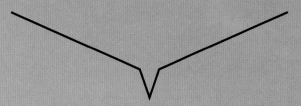

Steep dihedral, with very upswept wings: the plane is less likely to turn during flight.

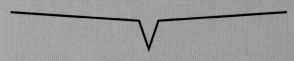

Shallow dihedral, wings not very upswept: the plane is more likely to turn during flight.

A plane with very upswept wings (steep dihedral) tends to turn much less than a glider with horizontal wings or wings angled down below the horizontal (anhedral). If you are having trouble making a particular plane fly straight, try bending the wings up to a more raised position.

Sometimes you will find that your plane rolls, or flies in a corkscrew path, and then crashes. This is often caused because the two wings are folded at

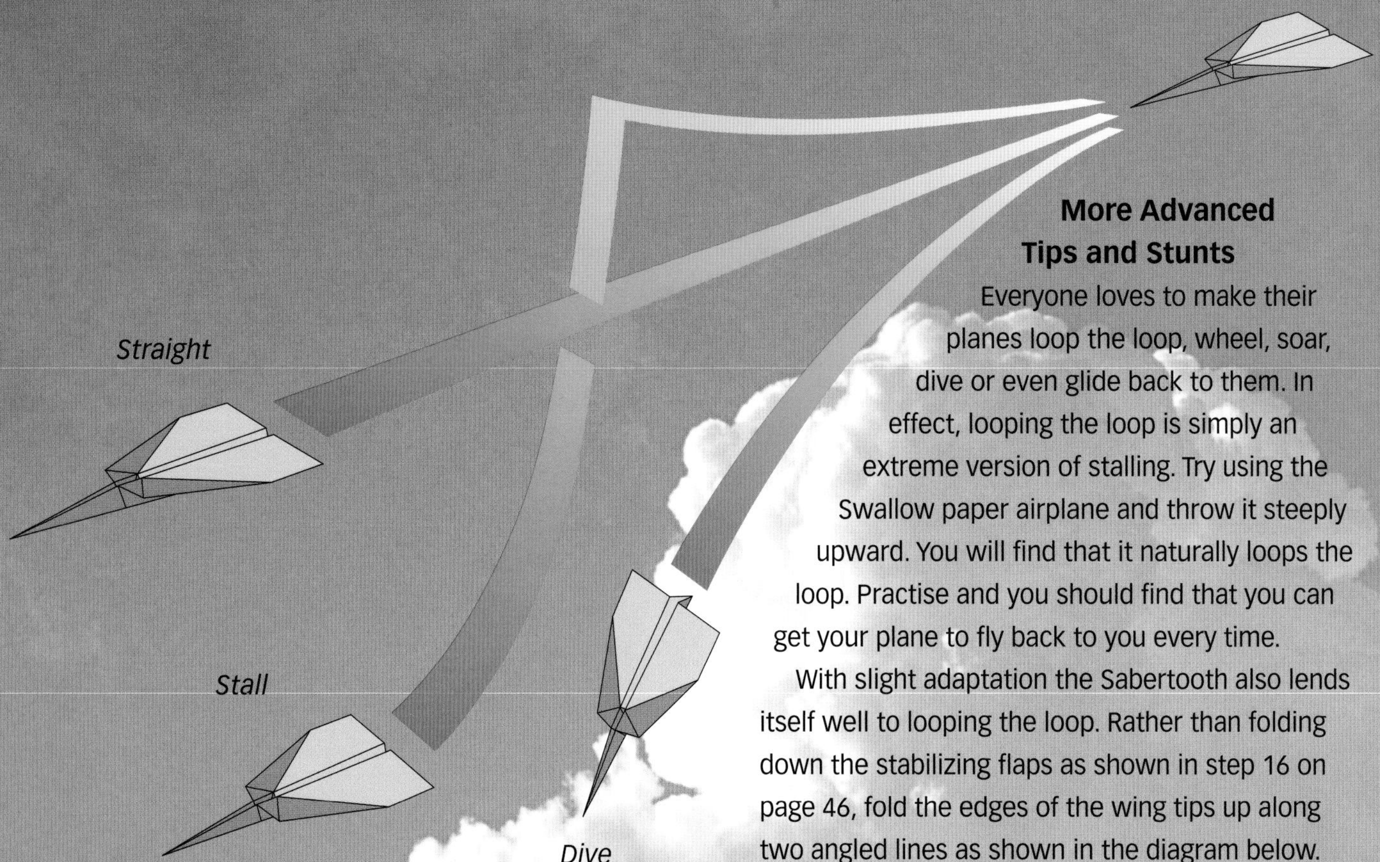

Straight

Stall

Dive

More Advanced Tips and Stunts

Everyone loves to make their planes loop the loop, wheel, soar, dive or even glide back to them. In effect, looping the loop is simply an extreme version of stalling. Try using the Swallow paper airplane and throw it steeply upward. You will find that it naturally loops the loop. Practise and you should find that you can get your plane to fly back to you every time.

With slight adaptation the Sabertooth also lends itself well to looping the loop. Rather than folding down the stabilizing flaps as shown in step 16 on page 46, fold the edges of the wing tips up along two angled lines as shown in the diagram below. Now throw the plane upwards quite hard and it will loop the loop.

different angles. Look carefully at your plane from the side and adjust the wings until they are entirely level. If the wings are level, check the rear of the wing surfaces. If one side is bent upwards or downwards and the other is straight or bent in the other direction, the plane will also spiral.

Some planes are also prone to stalling. Often this is caused by too much lift at the front of the plane which causes the nose to point up into the air. This means the plane loses speed, stops (the stall) and then falls nose-down out of the sky. It is usually quite simple to stop a plane from stalling. The easiest method is to slide a paper clip onto the nose. This stops the nose lifting up too far in the air causing the plane to stall. If a paper clip proves too heavy to let your plane fly, you can add a flap at the back of the plane.

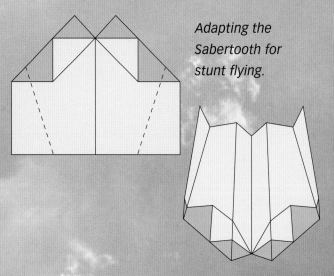

Adapting the Sabertooth for stunt flying.

This adaptation of the Sabertooth can also be applied to many of the paper airplanes shown in this book. Experiment and try this trick to see if you can make a unique stunt plane of your own.

GLIDERS

To qualify as a glider, a paper plane has to have special characteristics. Stable, slow and long-duration flight are the most important qualities of gliders. Modern fixed-wing flight was born from the study of paper gliders, hang gliders and kites in the 19th century. Even the Space Shuttle is a glider when it returns to Earth.

If you want to win a paper airplane flight duration competition or even break a world record, the best way to go about it is to experiment with designing a plane like the ones shown in this section.

CLASSIC DART

No book about paper airplanes could possibly be complete without this classic design. Most people know how to fold a simple paper dart like this, but here is a reminder of how to fold it accurately.

1 Start with a sheet of A4 paper and make a valley fold lengthways down the center of the sheet.

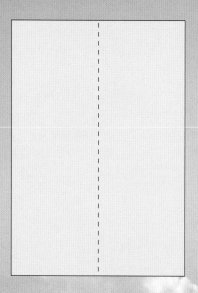

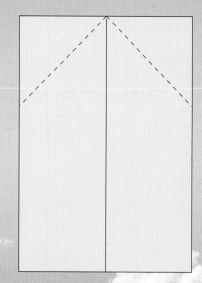

2 Now fold the top left and right corners in so that the left- and right-hand halves of the top edge lie squarely along the center line next to one another.

3 Fold the slanting top left- and right-hand edges in once more to lie along the center line.

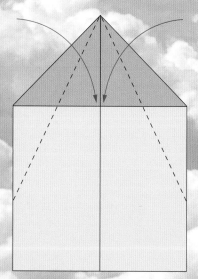

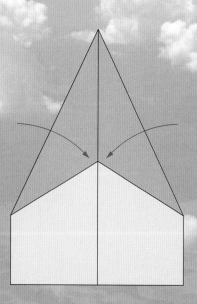

4 Crease these folds in carefully by running your thumbnail along them.

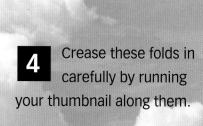

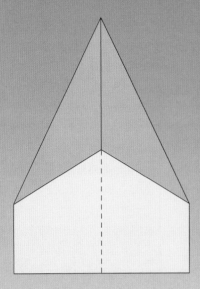

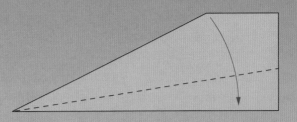

6 Fold one of the long, slanting folded edges down to align with the bottom edge of the center line. Turn the paper over and repeat the fold on the other side.

5 Now fold the plane in half along the center line so that the folded sections are on the inside of the model.

7 Open up the wings to create a slight upward angle (dihedral) when looking down the length of the plane from the nose.

TIP:
This is a fast glider with a sharp pointed nose. Be careful flying it. Launch it with its nose pointing slightly upwards and please avoid hitting people in their eyes and faces.

STEALTH BOMBER

This plane has a broad wing shape, similar to the B2 Stealth Bomber, and will silently glide a long distance indoors if thrown gently.

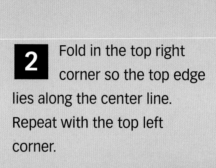

1 Start with a sheet of A4 paper and make a valley fold lengthways down the center.

2 Fold in the top right corner so the top edge lies along the center line. Repeat with the top left corner.

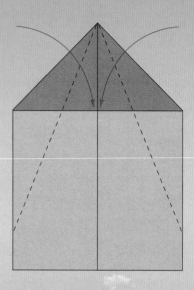

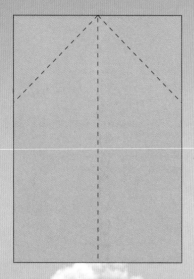

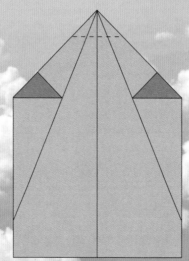

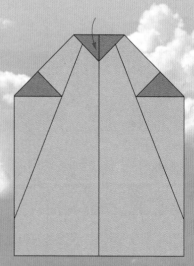

3 Now fold in the upper left-hand edge of the paper to lie along the center line and repeat with the upper right-hand edge.

4 Open out the sheet of paper so that it is at step 2 again. Fold the two triangular flaps back from the center, to align with the outer edges.

5 Fold the tip of the plane down to meet the center line about 2in (5cm) below the tip.

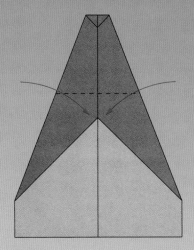

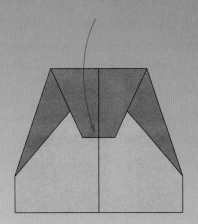

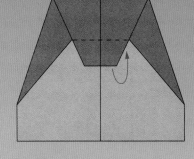

6 Now refold the paper along the lines that you created in step 3.

7 Fold down the blunt tip by about a further 3in (7.5cm) and crease the fold well.

8 Now make a fold in this flap about half way down its length and tuck the folded end underneath the flap and the folded-in edges. This helps to hold the plane together.

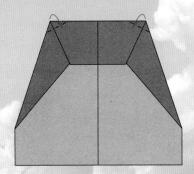

9 Now fold the top right- and left-hand points inwards by about ½in (1cm). These corners help to stabilize the paper airplane in flight.

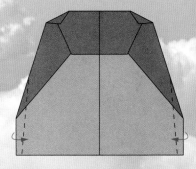

TIP:
This plane flies best if thrown gently and evenly. Try launching it outside on a still day to see how far it will glide.

10 Finally you will need some little winglets folded up or down at the ends of the wings. You may need to experiment with the size of these to find out what works best in practise.

RAPIER

A rapier is a light, thin sword and the name truly suits this sleek plane. It flies with the grace of a glider but has the accuracy and cutting edge of a dart. This plane truly gives you the best of both worlds and is really easy to make.

1 Start with a sheet of A4 paper and make a valley fold lengthways down the center of the sheet. Open up the paper again.

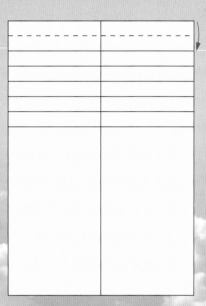

2 Fold the top ½in (1cm) of the sheet of paper downwards parallel with the bottom of the sheet. Now fold this top ½in (1cm) over again and repeat this action another four times.

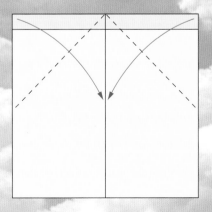

3 There will now be a heavy front lip at the top of a shortened sheet of paper. Fold the top left corner into the center line so that the top edge lies along the center line. Repeat with the top right corner. Fold the plane along the center line.

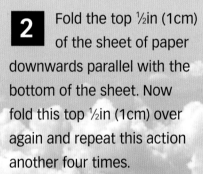

TIP:
Make your folds as clean, crisp and symmetrical as possible.

GLIDERS

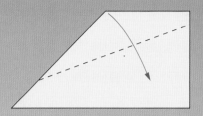

4 Fold down the wings. These should be folded along a diagonal line which runs from just above the nose of the plane to just below the corners at the rear. You should take into account the thick folds of paper at the front and not fold from the actual nose tip to avoid the paper splitting.

5 Open out the wings so that they are angled down just below the horizontal when you look along the plane from the nose.

VULCAN BOMBER

The Vulcan was a British nuclear bomber dating from the 1960s. It had a huge wingspan and a characteristic delta shape. When airborne, Vulcan bombers were an impressive sight as they droned across the sky. This plane borrows the shape of the Vulcan—get it right and you have an amazing glider in your hands.

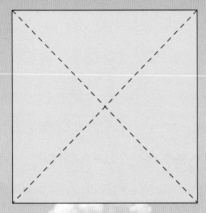

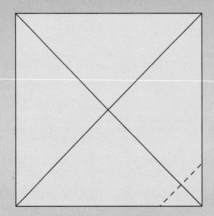

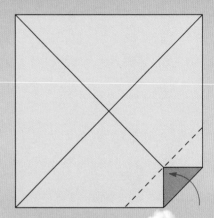

1 Shorten an A4 sheet of paper into a square (see page 11). Fold the paper along the diagonals joining the four corners of the square.

2 Now turn the sheet so that the bottom right-hand corner points towards you.

3 Fold this corner in to meet the diagonal at a point about one fifth of the distance to the center.

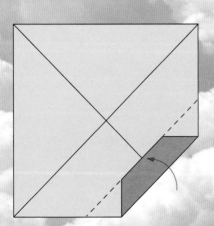

4 Fold in another section in the same way along a line running through the tip of the folded-in point and parallel to the first fold.

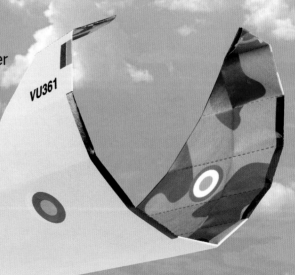

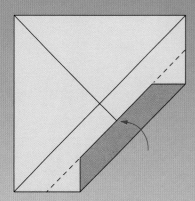

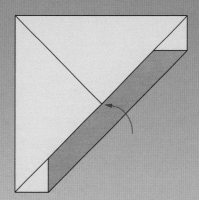

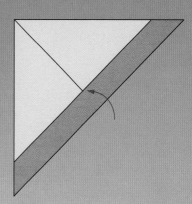

5 Now fold along the line formed by the folded-over edge created by the previous step.

6 Keep repeating this fold until the edge of your fold hits the diagonal line running from the top right to the bottom left of the square.

7 Make a final fold along the line of the diagonal. You are now left with a triangle which is exactly half the size of your original square sheet.

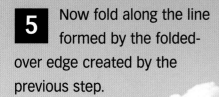

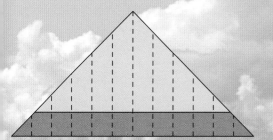

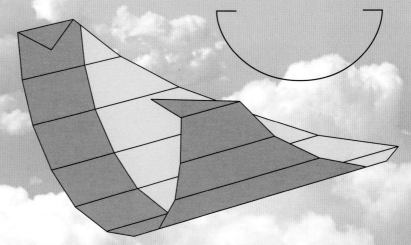

8 Now rotate the paper so that the folded strip is closest to you and the apex of the triangle points away from you. Fold it down the center line and then fold each half of the plane into six sections. In this step you should make a total of 11 folds.

9 Now open up the plane and give it the dihedral illustrated. Notice that the triangular outer sections on both ends have been folded in more acutely than the rest of the plane. They form two horizontal winglets that point inwards at each other.

SWALLOW

This plane not only looks great, it naturally loops, dives and circles back down to the ground if thrown steeply up into the air. Fly the Swallow outside on a warm, calm summer's day to show off its aerial abilities at their best.

1 Start with an A4 sheet of paper folded in half lengthways and then opened out again.

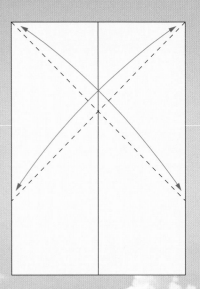

2 Fold the upper left-hand corner so that the top edge lies along the right-hand (longer) edge of the paper. Open up and repeat with the upper right-hand corner folding it down to the left-hand edge of the paper. Open up again.

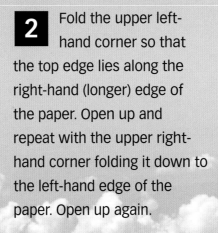

3 Turn over the paper keeping the diagonal creases at the top of the sheet. Fold the upper straight edge of the paper down to align with the lower points of the diagonal folds.

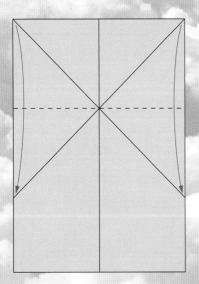

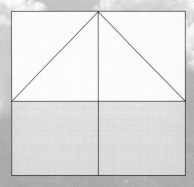

4 The fold will run through the point where the diagonals cross over one another. Crease hard and unfold.

GLIDERS

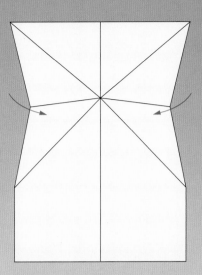

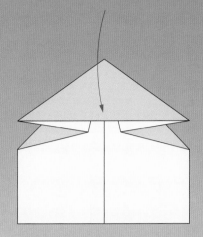

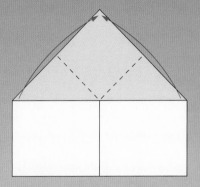

5 Turn over the paper again, grasp the ends of the horizontal crease, lift slightly and push them in towards the center.

6 Complete the fold so that the paper collapses back towards you as illustrated.

7 Fold the two loose points at the left and right of the top folded triangle upwards to meet at the topmost tip of the paper.

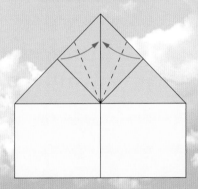

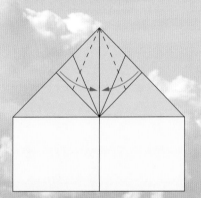

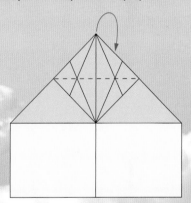

8 Fold in the bottom left edge of the diamond shape formed in the previous step so that it lies along the center line. Crease hard and repeat with the bottom right edge. Then unfold.

9 Do the same with the two upper edges of the diamond shape.

10 Now fold the top half of the diamond shape downwards so that it exactly overlaps the bottom half of the shape. Crease hard and unfold.

11 This is the tough bit! You should have a series of crossing creases in the diamond section at the nose of the plane. Fold both the edges of the right side of the diamond in to the center line again, but this time simultaneously! You should now have a flap standing straight up. Fold this down towards the tip and repeat these two steps for the left-hand side.

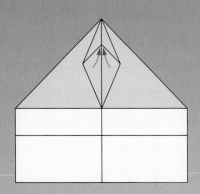

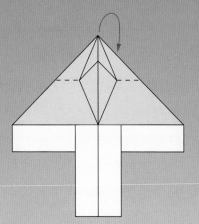

12 Now using a pair of scissors or a straight edge cut or tear off a strip from the unfolded bottom edge of the paper. It should be about 2in (5cm) wide.

13 Fold this lengthwise down its center line. Open it up and fold in the top left- and right-hand corners so their top edges lie along this center line in an arrow shape.

14 Push this tip inside the pocket of the plane so the "arrowhead" of the strip lies snugly inside the nose of the plane and the center creases match exactly. Now turn the plane over and fold the tip back along the line created in step 10.

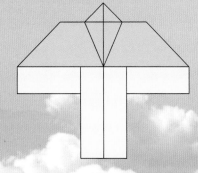

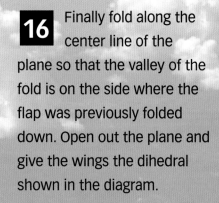

15 This should trap the tip of the tail inside the plane and give it a pointed nose.

16 Finally fold along the center line of the plane so that the valley of the fold is on the side where the flap was previously folded down. Open out the plane and give the wings the dihedral shown in the diagram.

FIGHTERS

These paper airplanes are sleek and streamlined. They are designed to look like supersonic fighter aircraft which have an aggressive delta shape to reduce drag when they are flying at more than the speed of sound.

Try them when taking part in distance or target-shooting competitions. They are easy to make and easy to fly. Be careful though—they are sharp. Don't hit anyone in the eye with those pointed noses!

F-14 TOMCAT

The wings of the real F-14 Tomcat can move backwards and forwards—when they are in full swept-back mode, they merge into the tail. This paper airplane captures the angular beauty of the Tomcat and is ideal to adapt for aerial acrobatics—especially barrel rolls.

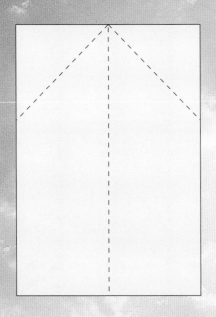

1 Start with a sheet of A4 paper, creased in half lengthways in a mountain fold.

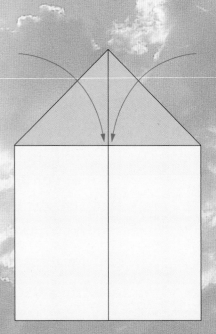

2 Fold in the top right corner so that the edge of the paper lies along the center line. Repeat with the top left corner.

3 Now fold down the point that you have produced towards you, making the crease along the base of the triangle.

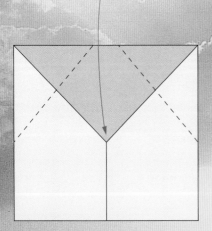

4 Fold down the new top left and top right corners so that they meet at a point on the center line about 3in (7.5cm) below the top edge.

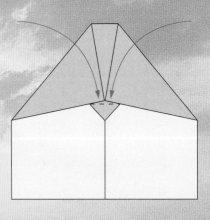

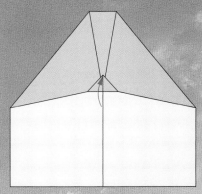

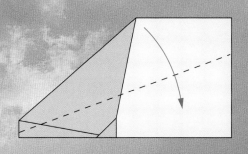

5 Fold the little triangle of paper sticking out below this point back up over the flaps created in step 4. This technique was created by paper planes expert Eiji Nakamura.

6 Refold the plane along the center mountain crease. Check that the plane is symmetrical at this point. The small triangle you folded up in step 5 should hold the plane together securely. Fold down the wing along a line stretching from just above the nose to a point on the back edge about 1in (2.5cm) in from the top corner.

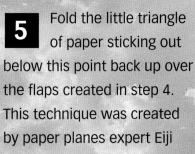

7 Crease the fold firmly, then turn the paper over and match the fold on the other wing. Open out the wings so that their angle is slightly above the horizontal.

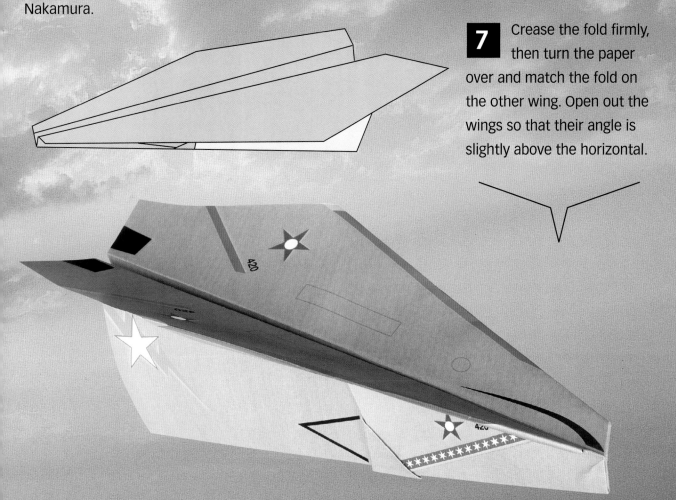

DRAKEN

The Draken is a sleek fighter with a futuristic shape. It was originally designed for the Swedish government in 1949. The plane has a double delta-shaped wing and is capable of reaching Mach 2 (twice the speed of sound). The paper model can't manage that, but it does mimic the fantastic shape of the Draken.

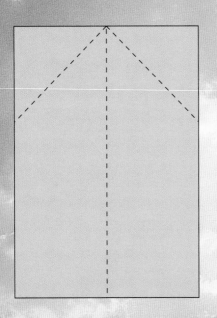

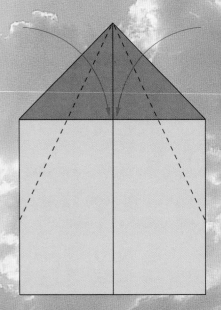

1 Start with a sheet of A4 paper and make a valley fold lengthways down the center line.

2 Fold in the top two corners so that they lie along the center crease.

3 Fold in the newly created slanting edges to meet along the center line and crease them.

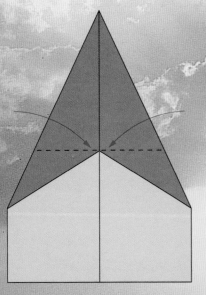

4 Fold the tip of the plane down so that it meets the center point of the bottom edge of the paper.

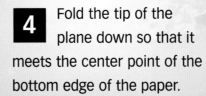

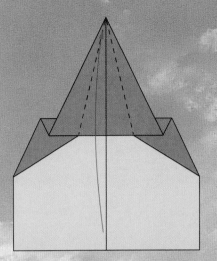
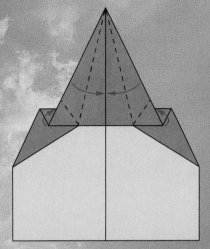

5 Now fold this flap up again along a line about 1in (2.5cm) below the fold created in step 4.

6 Fold the two edges of this new narrow triangle in to the center line again. This is tricky as you will find it lifts up two flaps (see detail diagram). These must be folded over and pressed flat to complete the fold.

7 Re-crease the plane following its center line and fold down the wings behind the nose along the lines that are made by the edges of the angled nose.

8 Open up the model and lift the wings so that they are slightly above the horizontal.

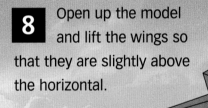

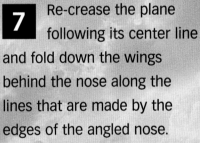

DRAKEN
WITH AFTERBURNER

Once you have made the Draken model, you can adapt it to create a Draken with afterburner. When the pilot engages the afterburner this produces a great plume of flame from the jet exhaust. This creates extra thrust and accelerates the aircraft all the way to Mach 2.

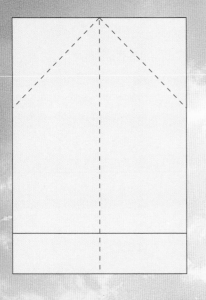

1 Start with a sheet of A4 paper that has been shortened by about 2in (5cm). Mark the paper's center line lengthways by making a crease along it and then opening it out.

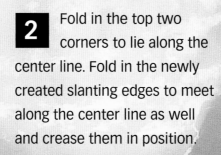

2 Fold in the top two corners to lie along the center line. Fold in the newly created slanting edges to meet along the center line as well and crease them in position.

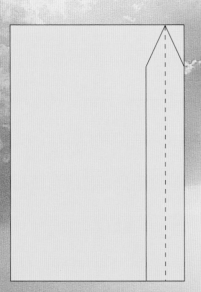

3 Now take another sheet of A4 paper and trim off a 2in (5cm) wide strip from one long side of the paper. Fold it down its center lengthwise and trim the point into an arrow shape that exactly matches the shape of the tip of your plane.

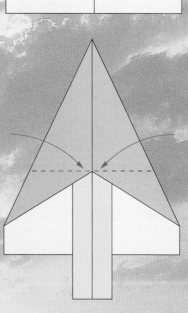

4 Slide this strip of paper up the center of the plane under the flap so that it lies inside the folded-over nose.

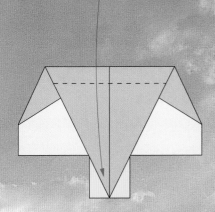

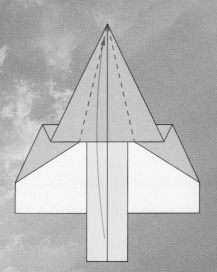

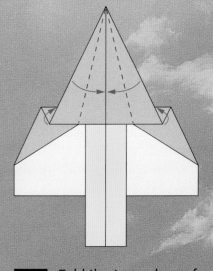

5 Fold the tip of the plane down to the bottom of the tail, thereby trapping the tail inside the plane.

6 Now fold this flap back up again along a line about 1in (2.5cm) below the fold created in step 5.

7 Fold the two edges of this new narrow triangle in to the center line again. This is tricky as you will find it lifts up two flaps. These must be folded over and pressed flat to complete the fold. This is the same as fold 6 of the Draken.

8 Re-crease the plane following its center line and fold down the wings behind the nose along the lines that are made by the edges of the angled nose.

9 Open up and lift the wings to a position slightly above the horizontal. The extra tail section looks like the spurt of flame from an afterburner.

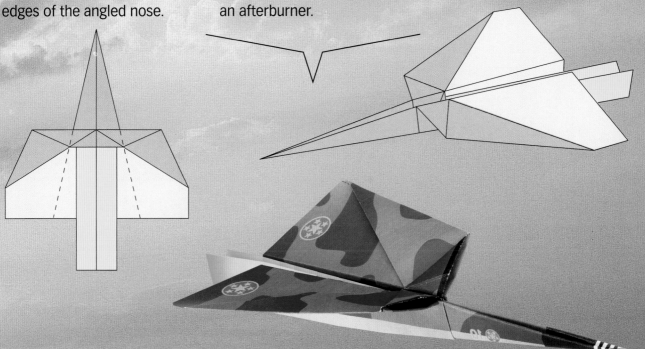

DELTA DART F-106

This paper airplane is fast and furious. Throw it hard and watch it go! The Delta Dart F-106 fighter aircraft which inspired this design was capable of flying faster than twice the speed of sound. As the name suggests, it had a sharply angled delta shape that this model picks up on.

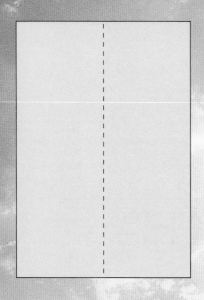

1 Start with a sheet of A4 paper and make a mountain fold lengthways down its center.

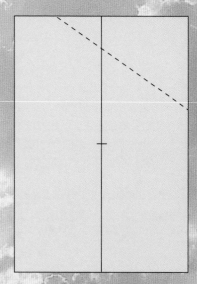

2 Pinch a point halfway along this line to mark the center of the sheet.

3 Fold the top right corner of the paper down to touch this point.

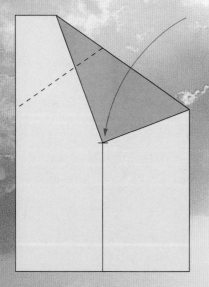

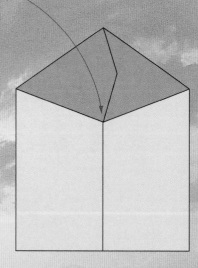

4 Now fold the top left corner in the same way to touch this point as well.

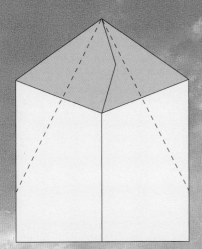

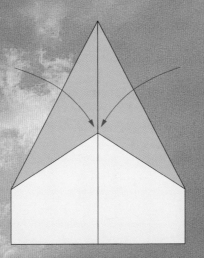

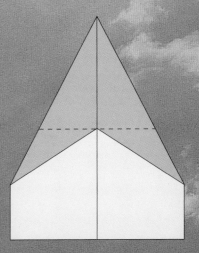

5 You are now going to fold the top left and top right corners of the sheet into the center line.

6 Fold in the slanting top left- and right-hand edges so that they lie precisely next to one another along the center line.

7 You will have made a dart shape as shown in this diagram.

TIP:
This plane requires some tight folding, so try using lighter stock than normal copier or printer paper.

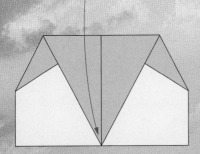

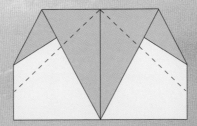

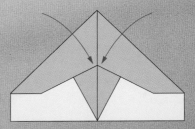

8 Fold the tip of the dart shape down to touch the center line on the bottom edge. This fold should lie exactly half way up the original sheet.

9 The next step is to fold the top left- and right-hand points in towards the center line.

10 The short top left- and right-hand edges now lie next to one another along the center line.

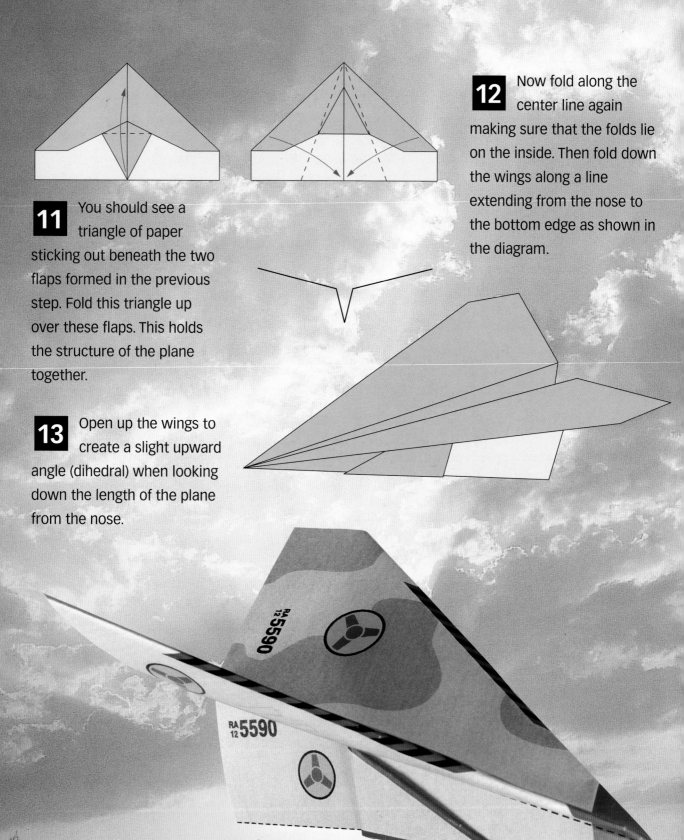

11 You should see a triangle of paper sticking out beneath the two flaps formed in the previous step. Fold this triangle up over these flaps. This holds the structure of the plane together.

12 Now fold along the center line again making sure that the folds lie on the inside. Then fold down the wings along a line extending from the nose to the bottom edge as shown in the diagram.

13 Open up the wings to create a slight upward angle (dihedral) when looking down the length of the plane from the nose.

WEIRD AND WONDERFUL

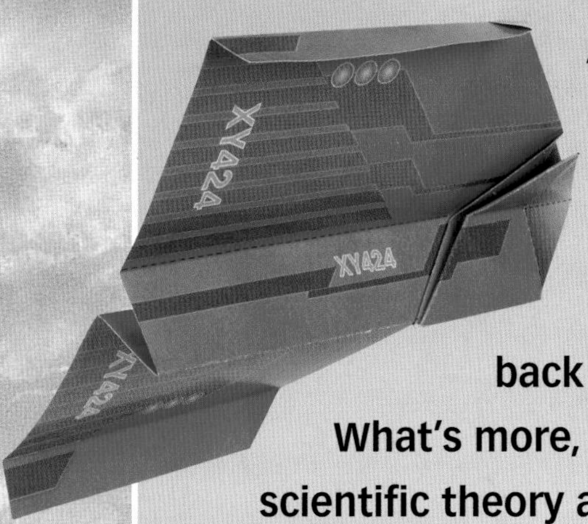

A plane that is simply a cylinder, a paper helicopter and other weird designs can be found in this section. These planes push back the boundaries of the hobby. What's more, they are all based on sound scientific theory and really show you what can be achieved with just a sheet of paper.

Experiment yourself and see what you can create. Who knows? You might design the next world-record breaker!

ORIGAMI PLANE

Like many origami models, this paper airplane is made using a square of paper. To fly at its best, the plane needs to be launched hard from your hand and pointing very slightly downwards.

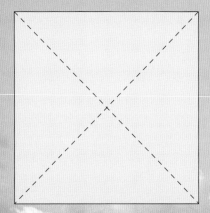

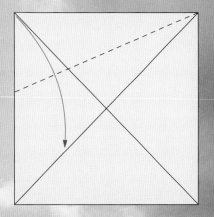

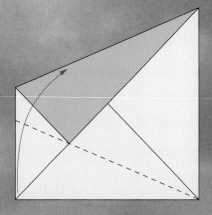

1 Shorten an A4 sheet of paper into a square (see page 11 for instructions on how to do this). Draw in the diagonals on your square of paper.

2 Fold down the top left corner so that the top edge of the paper lies along the diagonal running from the top right- to bottom left-hand corner and crease.

3 Then fold in the bottom edge to lie along the line of the other diagonal.

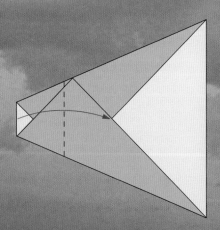

4 Fold the left edge (the nose) in so its center point lies exactly on the center point of the original square of paper.

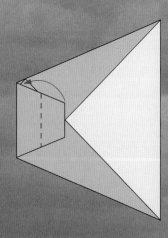

5 Now fold this flap of paper in half again crossways and tuck this fold underneath.

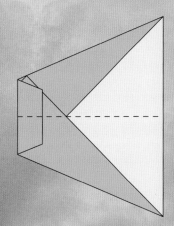

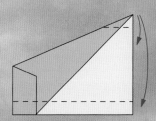

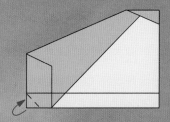

6 Fold the entire model along the center line of the plane.

7 Now fold down the wings on either side and also fold down some small winglets at the ends of the wings.

8 Fold over the tip of the nose section to make a crease and then push it inwards so that it tucks back on itself. This improves stability and helps to prevent stalls.

9 Open out the plane and allow the wings to droop a little below the horizontal (dihedral).

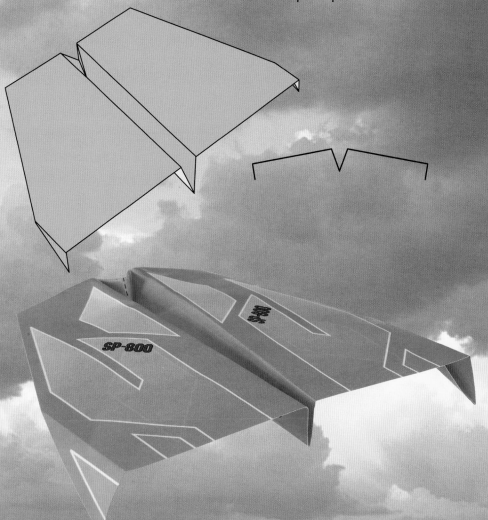

TIP:
Launch this plane hard and pointing slightly down and it will reward you with a long, slow descent. It may be one of the simplest planes in the book, but it is also one of the best.

MITER

Bishops wear miters on their heads and this paper airplane borrows that look. It shows how a simple, but extremely unusual, design can fly well. Throw it slightly upwards for best results. If this plane doesn't convince you to start experimenting with your own designs, nothing will!

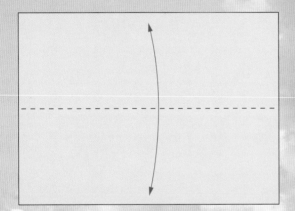 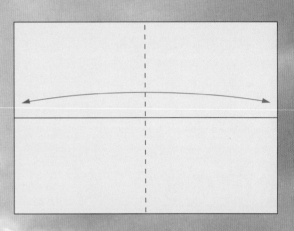

1 Find the center of a sheet of A4 paper by folding it in half lengthways, opening it out and then folding in half crossways. The point where the two folds intersect is the center.

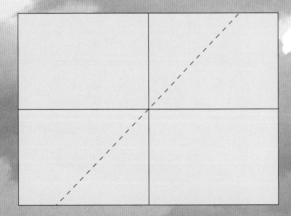

2 Fold the sheet diagonally (at 45°) through the center point of the paper (where the two folds cross).

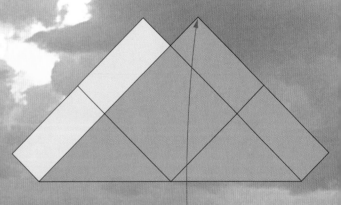

3 This aligns the bottom edge of the paper with the left-hand edge. When you turn the paper so that it is in the position shown in the diagram, the top two points should be at the same height.

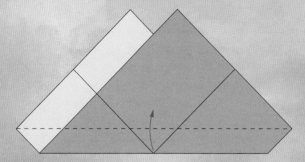

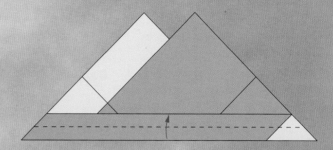

4 Now fold the bottom edge upwards. This fold should be made crisply along the line joining the points at the left- and right-hand sides of the paper.

5 You will have a thick strip along the bottom. Now fold this strip in half again so that the two edges line up exactly.

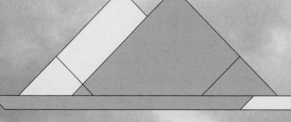

6 This fold will produce a corner piece sticking out at each side.

7 Roll this form into a tight cylinder with the thickened edge on the inside of the roll. The model will resemble a bishop's miter.

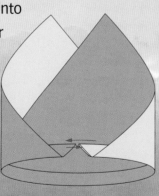

8 Now let the cylinder relax and tuck the left-hand corner of the folded strip produced in step 6 into the right-hand end forming an open cylinder. Don't get frustrated if your cylinder keeps unravelling because the tucked-in pieces slip out. Cheat and use some sticky tape!

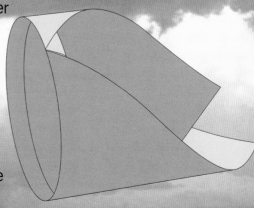

TIP:
Launch this model gently, releasing the plane horizontal to the ground with the two points nearer the ground facing backwards and the narrow section— where it is joined into a loop—on top.

MAKING PAPER PLANES

U2 SPY PLANE

This is the most aerodynamically perfect paper airplane in the book. With a wide wingspan and narrow wings, it has a low aspect ratio—the distance from the front of the wing to the back of the wing divided by the wingspan. This is what is needed for the best gliding flight, as it produces the least drag. In this respect it is very like America's high-flying, top-secret U2 spy plane.

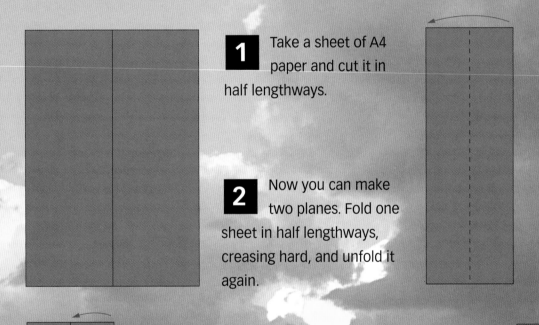

1 Take a sheet of A4 paper and cut it in half lengthways.

2 Now you can make two planes. Fold one sheet in half lengthways, creasing hard, and unfold it again.

3 Fold in the right-hand long edge so that it lies upon the center line folded in the previous step.

4 Now you will have a fresh fold on the right-hand edge. Fold this to lie along the edge of the paper folded in to the center in the previous step.

WEIRD AND WONDERFUL

5 Then fold the paper along the original center line.

6 This fold turns the thick strip over onto the left-hand half of the paper.

7 Turn the paper over. Make a crease half way along the folded long side of this flying-wing shape. This crease should be at right angles to the edge and only extend half way across the wing.

8 This will result in a sharp crease in the nose, but no crease at the back. The back will still have a rounded form due to the V-shape created at the front.

TIP:
Launch the plane gently. It will glide slowly and sedately with little drag.

HELICOPTER

For something a bit more wacky, try this classic paper toy. Drop it and watch it spiral down to the ground like an airborne sycamore seed. You can even race one against a friend's—the winner is the one that stays in the air longer.

1 Take a sheet of A4 paper and trim off a 2in (5cm) wide strip from one long side of the paper. Cut the paper according to the diagram—the solid lines show where you should cut.

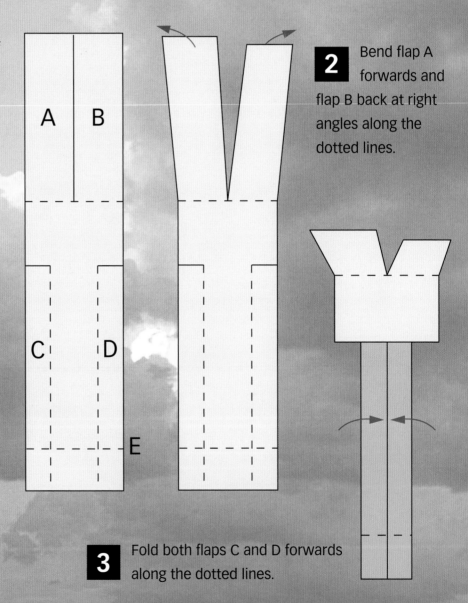

2 Bend flap A forwards and flap B back at right angles along the dotted lines.

3 Fold both flaps C and D forwards along the dotted lines.

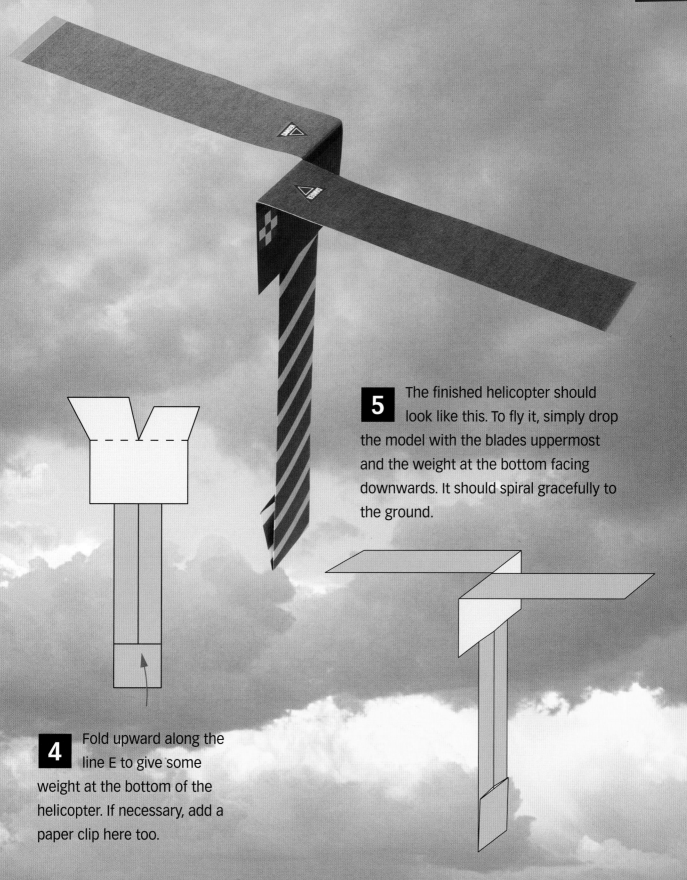

5 The finished helicopter should look like this. To fly it, simply drop the model with the blades uppermost and the weight at the bottom facing downwards. It should spiral gracefully to the ground.

4 Fold upward along the line E to give some weight at the bottom of the helicopter. If necessary, add a paper clip here too.

SABERTOOTH

This plane has a double fuselage and a two-pronged nose. It is one of the best gliders I know and is probably the most complicated plane to make in the book. Once you have mastered this design, you will be able fold almost any other paper airplane.

1 Start with a sheet of A4 paper in portrait alignment (with the short sides at the top and bottom) and crease it in half lengthways to form a valley fold.

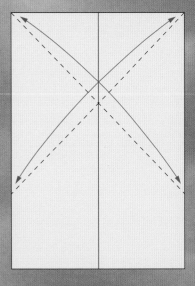

2 Fold down the top right corner so that the top edge aligns with the left-hand side. Crease hard and unfold. Repeat with the upper left corner folded to the opposite side.

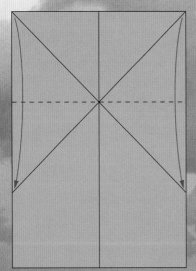

3 Flip the paper over keeping the top corners still at the top. Fold down the top edge on a horizontal line that passes through the point where the diagonal creases intersect.

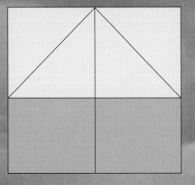

4 Crease hard along this line, unfold and flip the paper back to the starting position.

WEIRD AND WONDERFUL

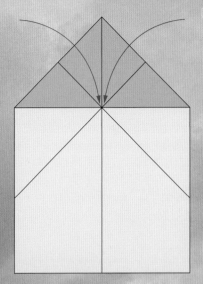

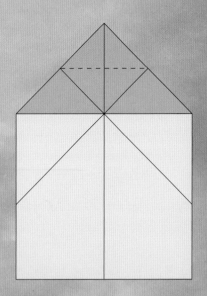

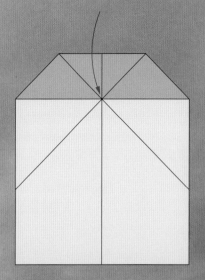

5 Now fold down the top right and top left corners so that they meet at the intersection of the two diagonal folds and crease hard.

6 Fold down the tip of the triangle formed by the two diagonal folds.

7 The triangle's tip should touch the intersection point of the two diagonal folds.

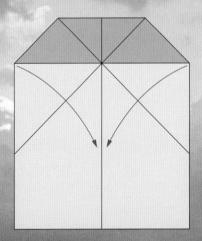

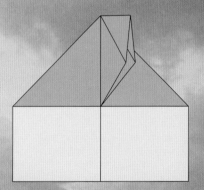

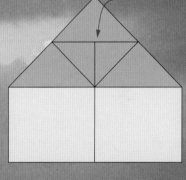

9 This should create a vertical flap as shown in the diagram.

10 Now open this flap outwards and press it flat along the existing diagonal creases.

8 This is the first complex step. Pull the ends of the horizontal crease formed in step 3 towards the center valley fold.

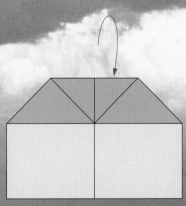

11 Fold the small triangular pocket at the top of the plane down underneath the model.

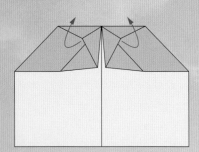

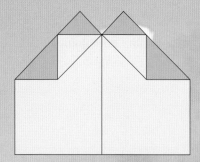

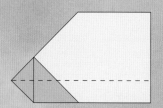

12 Aha! The second complex step. Hold the plane flat on your work surface so that the flap underneath (step 11) cannot move. Place a finger inside each of the small triangular flaps and pull them upwards and forwards.

13 Then press the flaps flat, creasing hard, to form a design which has two triangular points at the front.

14 Nearly finished! Fold along the center valley fold again. Turn the plane sideways and fold down the top side along a line running parallel with the long edge of the plane and passing through the point of the triangular tip on this side.

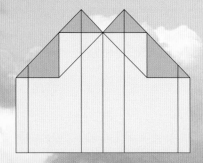

15 Turn over and repeat on the other side. Looking from above, you should end up with a shape like this.

16 Open out the wings and angle them just below the horizontal. Fold down the outer ½in (1cm) of the wings to add stability.

COMPETITION FLYING

There are three main categories of paper airplane performance for which world records can be established: time aloft, distance covered and size. All flight competitions must be held indoors. This is to ensure still air and calm conditions. A gust of wind could easily create a false record by carrying a plane high up into the air, or dash the hopes of an excellent design by blowing it off course into a wall or the ground.

For a Guinness world record, each competitor is allowed ten attempts in one session and these must be observed by two independent scrutineers who are persons of "good character".

Time Aloft

This is quite simply the time from the moment when the plane leaves the thrower's hand until it first touches the floor.

To get the best time, you really need to throw the plane straight upwards to give it lots of initial height. It should then level out and, if you have adjusted it correctly with a very slight asymmetry, it will describe a wide, slow turning circle as it descends to the floor. The size of the turning circle is critical: you don't want the plane to hit the wall (too wide) or to spiral out of control (too narrow). The fine adjustments to the set-up of the plane are the key to the success of such great paper airplane professionals as the current world record holder, Ken Blackburn. You will find details of his record on page 48.

Distance

For this world record a line is marked in a large arena or sports hall from behind which each competitor must throw their plane. The distance recorded is the measurement from this line to the point where the plane first touches the floor.

The best results are achieved by planes which fly in a straight line. Again the real professionals achieve their results by adjusting the plane perfectly. You don't want your plane to fly a vast distance but to land at your feet because it flew in a circle. You can win this record with a long gliding flight or by just throwing very hard and hoping for the best. A combination of both approaches often wins.

My favorite type of distance competition is not a world record class. It involves releasing the plane from a fixed height with no forward thrust allowed.

This shows which designs are the best gliders and eliminates any strength advantage from the throw, so that children can compete on equal terms with adults.

Size

This is measured in terms of the largest wingspan of a plane flown indoors over a distance of 50ft (15.24m). The current record wingspan is 40ft 10in (12.45m) and this was set by a team of students from the Faculty of Aerospace Engineering at Delft University in the Netherlands on 16th May 1995. Before this, the record was held by schoolchildren from Hampton, Virginia, USA. You may only use glue and paper to build the airplane—no special materials are needed—so anyone can have a go.

RULES AND RECORDS

Time aloft record holders

Guinness World Record: 27.6sec set by Ken Blackburn, 8th October 1998
Guinness British Record: 20.9sec set by Chris Edge and Andy Currey, 28th July 1996

Distance record holders

Guinness World Record: 58.82m (193ft) Tony Fletch, 21st May 1985
Guinness British Record: 31.7m (104ft) Andy Currey, 19th September 1997

Rules

There are many rules governing the time aloft and distance records. The most important are listed below.

• Only one sheet of paper may be used (A4 or US writing paper) and this paper may weigh no more than 100gsm.
• Adhesive tape measuring up to 25mm by 30mm may be cut up into as many small strips as required which may be used to hold down folds, but not for adding weight or improving aerodynamics.
• No glue is allowed.

• The paper can be cut but no cut piece may be rejoined.
• If the plane touches anything during the flight, the attempt is deemed void (even if it hits a wire).
• The plane must be thrown by one person and without using a long run-up.
• The thrower must not allow their feet to leave the ground intentionally or be on a raised platform during the throw.
• A maximum of ten attempts are allowed at one session.
• Distance throwers must not touch or cross over the launching line.

Useful contacts

• Learn more paper airplane designs from the writer of this book at www.paperairplanes.co.uk
• If you are inspired to know more about fluids and aerodynamics, a good starting point is the image gallery at www.efluids.com
• Andy Chipling who is deeply involved in setting the Guinness World Record rules has a website explaining the rules in full at www.paperaircraft.com

Classic Dart

Fold 2

Fold 3

Fold 4

Fold 5

Folds 1 and 6

01

Fold 8

Fold 7

01

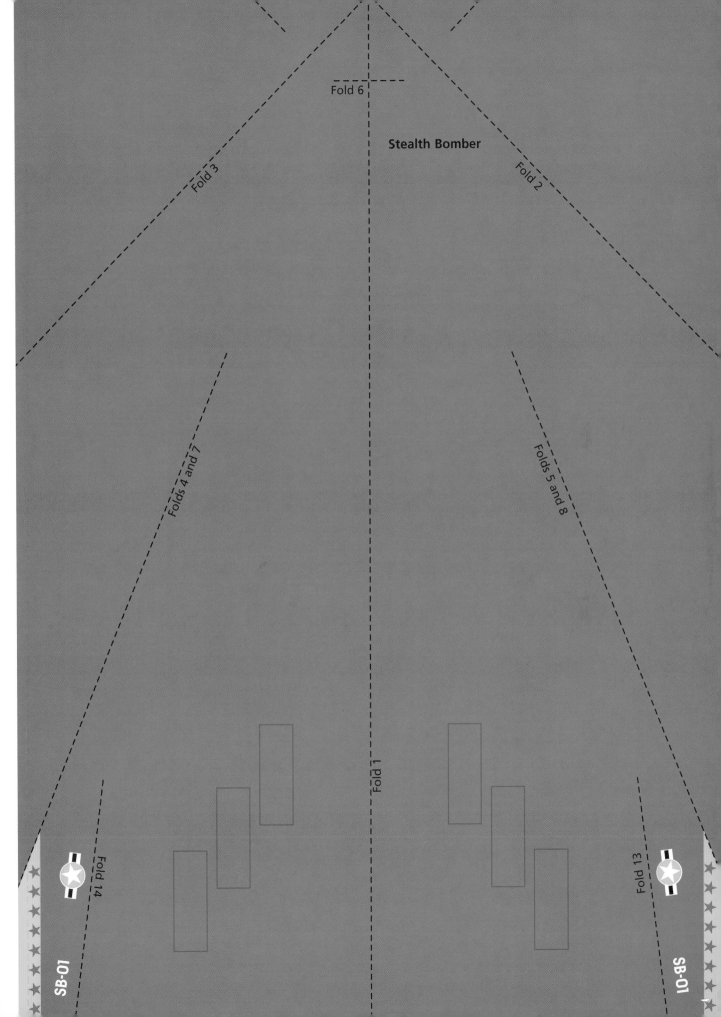

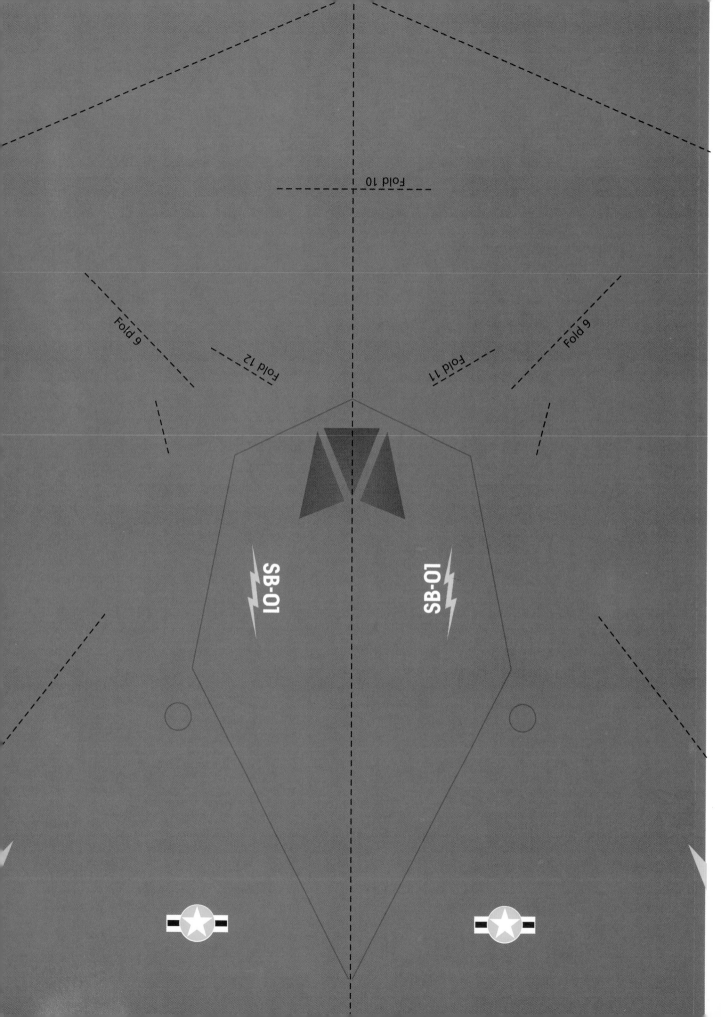

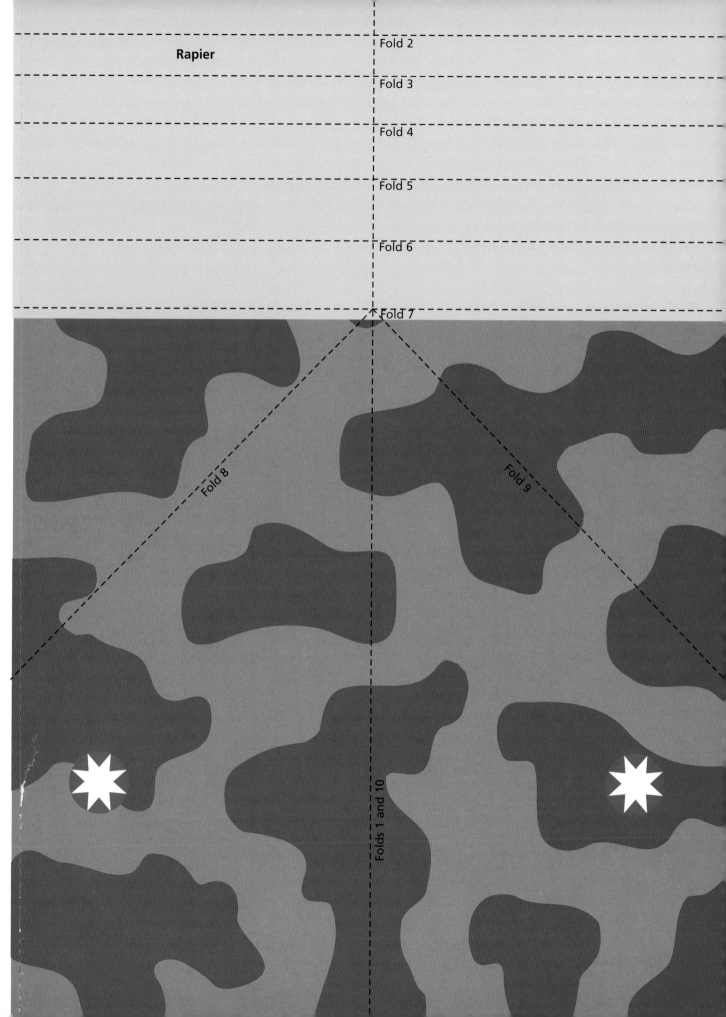

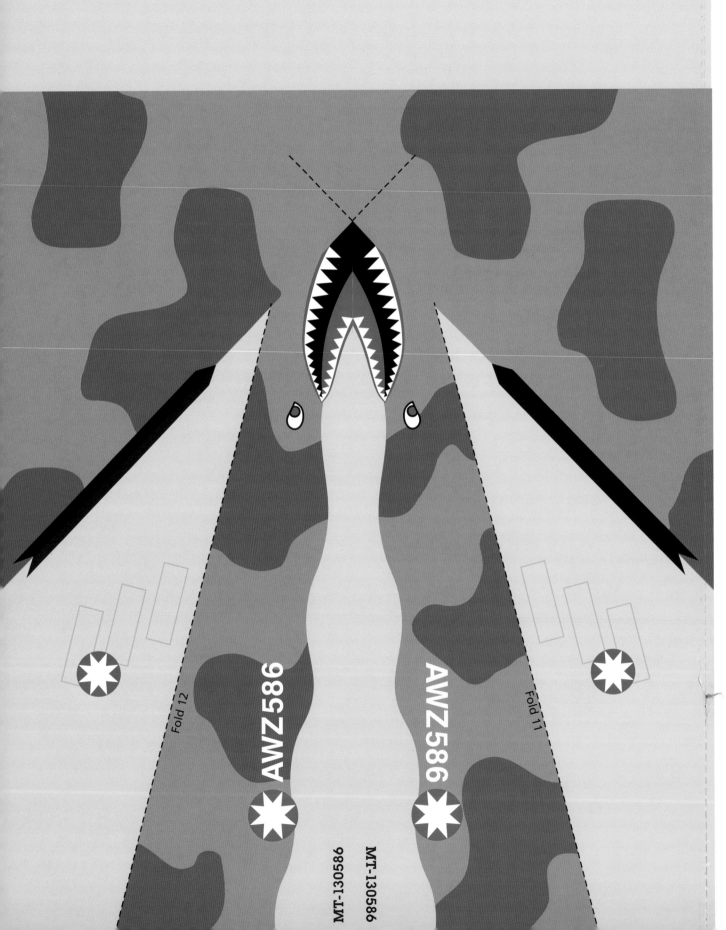

Fold 12

Fold 11

AWZ586

AWZ586

MT-130586

MT-130586

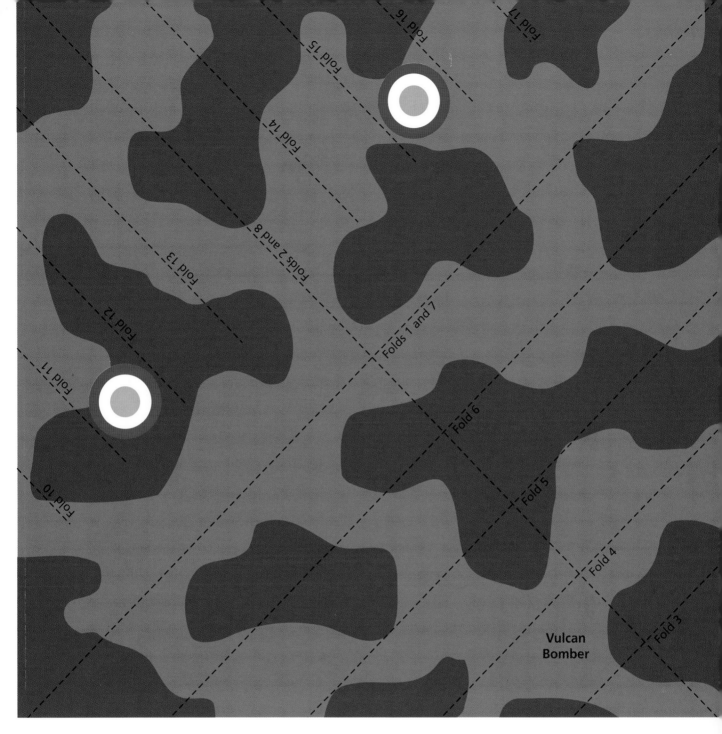

Folds 1 and 7

Fold 3

Fold 4

Fold 5

Fold 6

Folds 2 and 8

Fold 10

Fold 11

Fold 12

Fold 13

Fold 14

Fold 15

Fold 16

Fold 17

Vulcan
Bomber

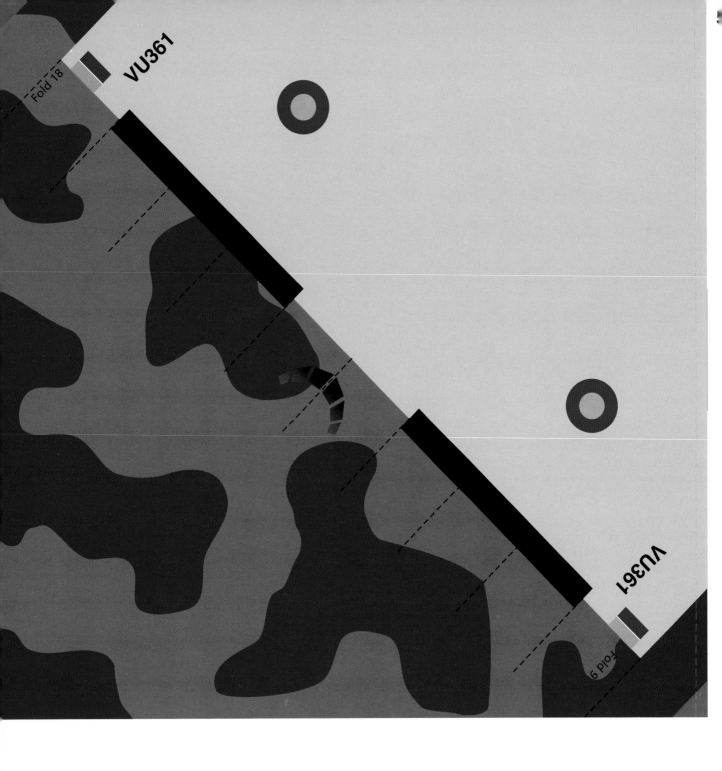

Fold 18

VU361

VU361

Fold 9

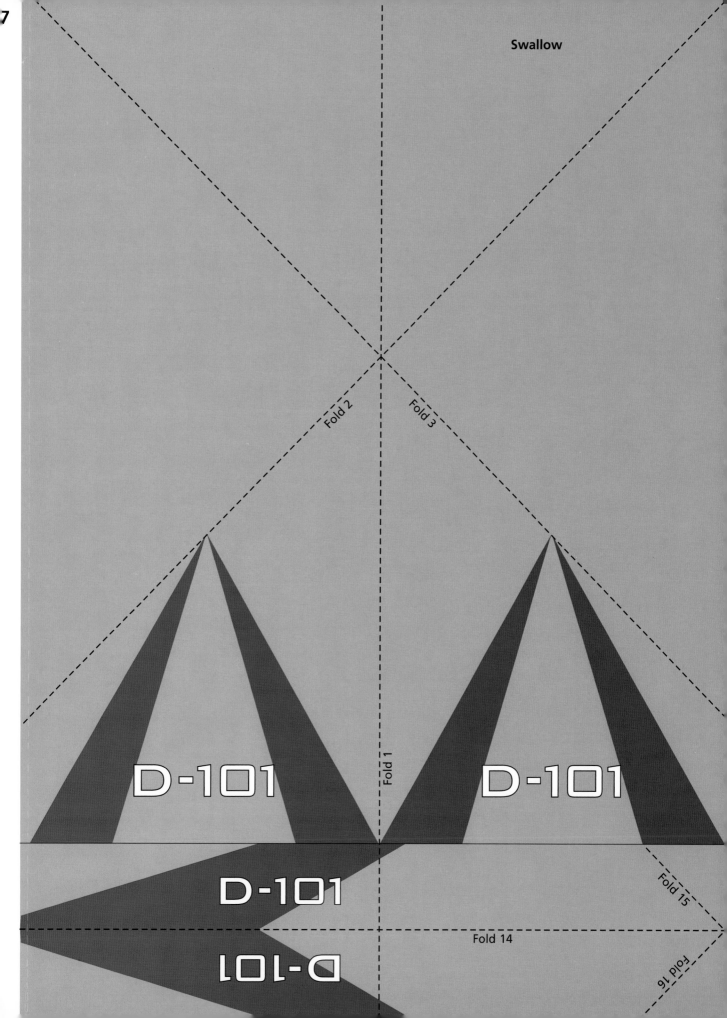

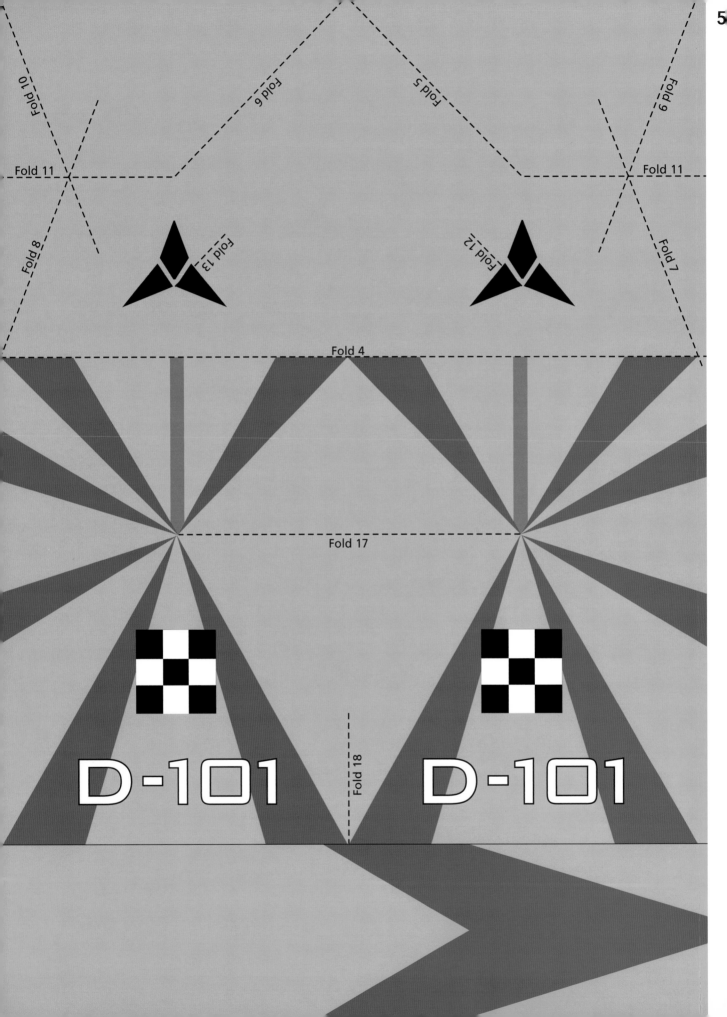

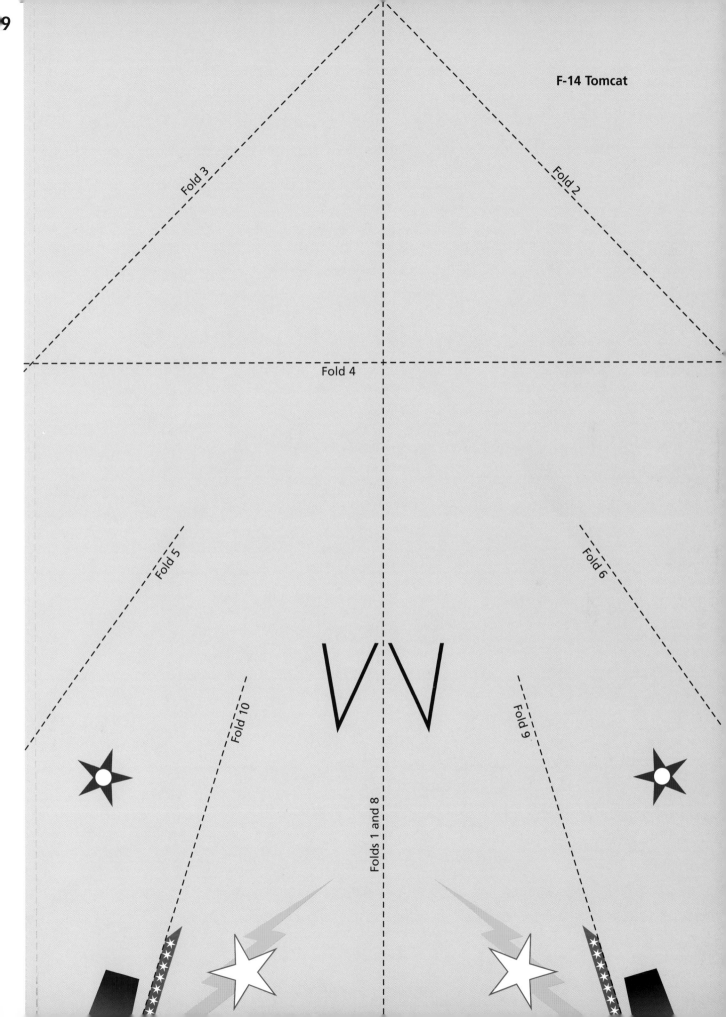

F-14 Tomcat

Fold 3

Fold 2

Fold 4

Fold 5

Fold 6

Fold 10

Fold 9

Folds 1 and 8

Fold 7

420

420

420

420

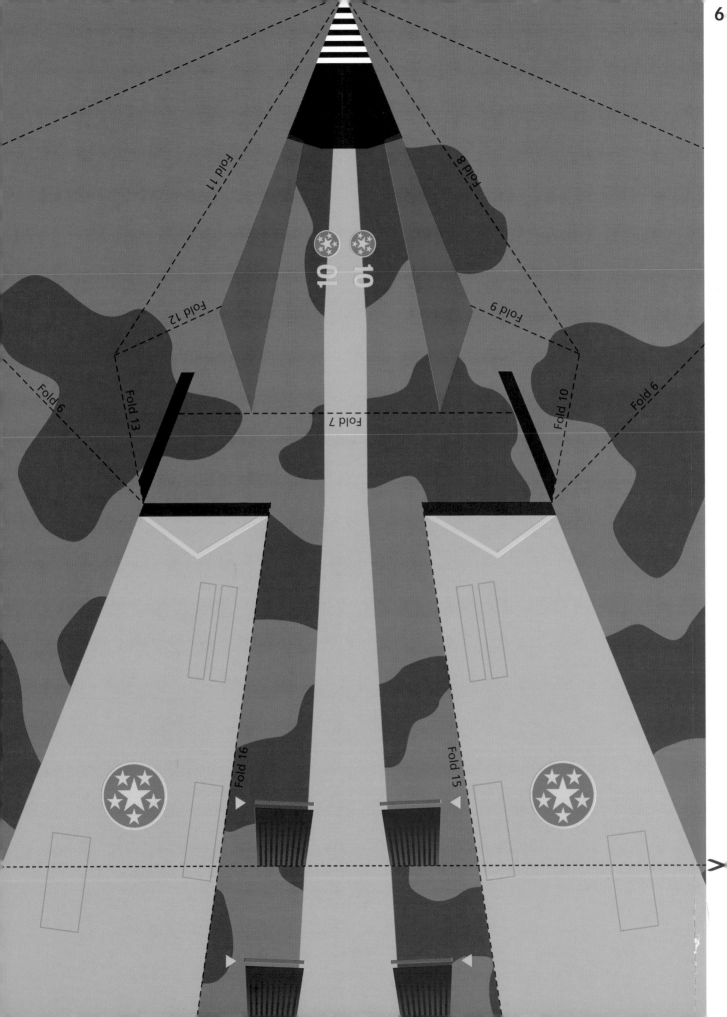

Carefully cut along dotted lines to separate models.

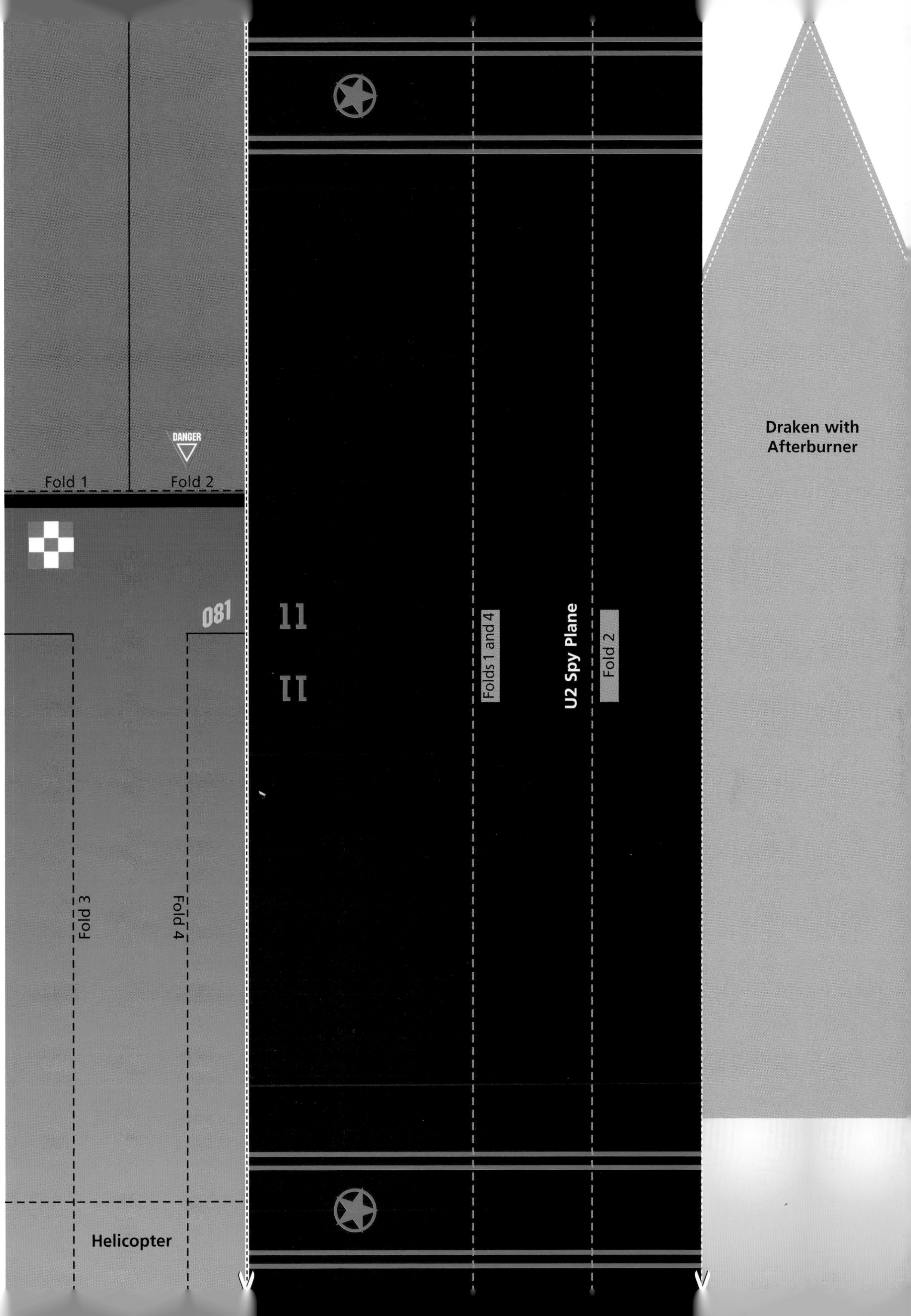
DANGER
Fold 1
Fold 2
081
Fold 3
Fold 4
Helicopter
11
11
Folds 1 and 4
U2 Spy Plane
Fold 2
Draken with
Afterburner

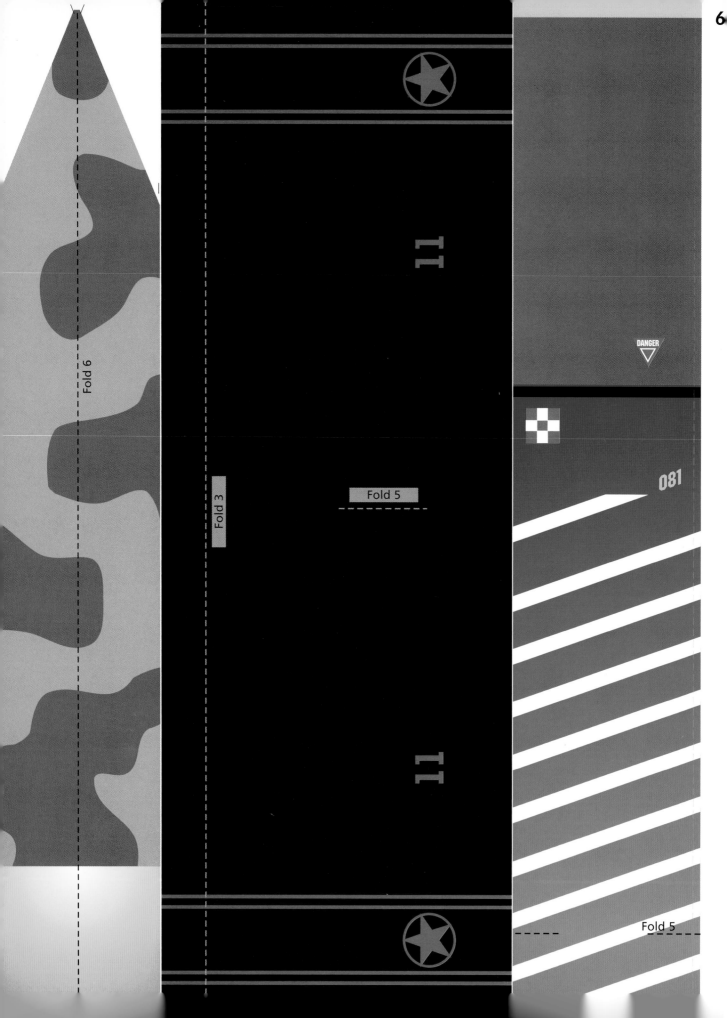

Fold 6

Fold 3

Fold 5

11

11

DANGER

081

Fold 5

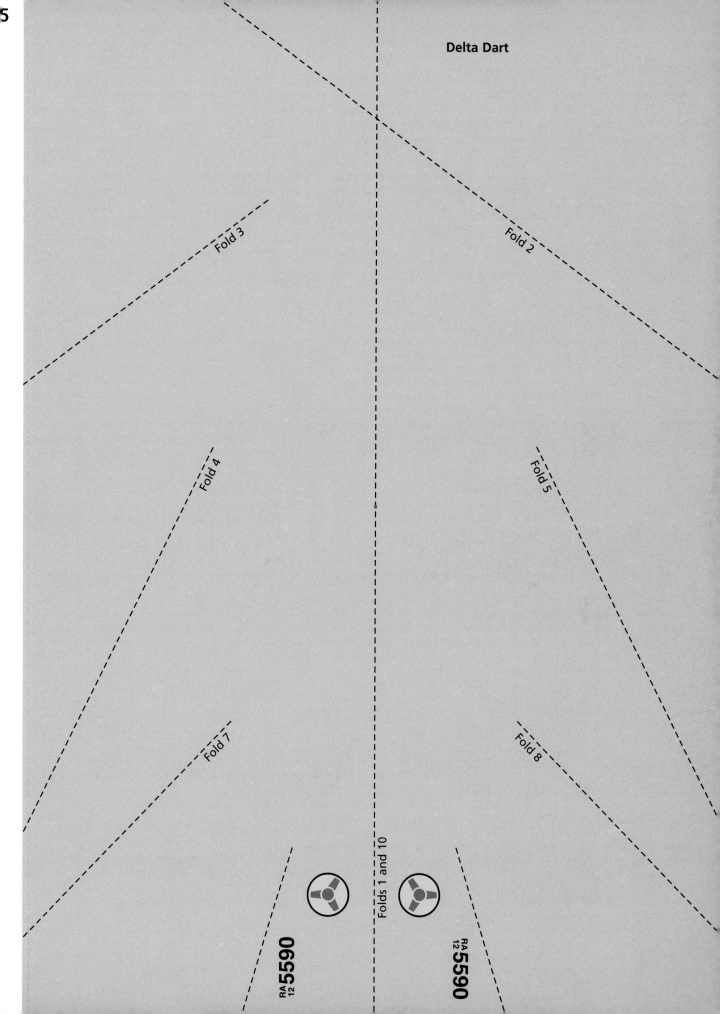

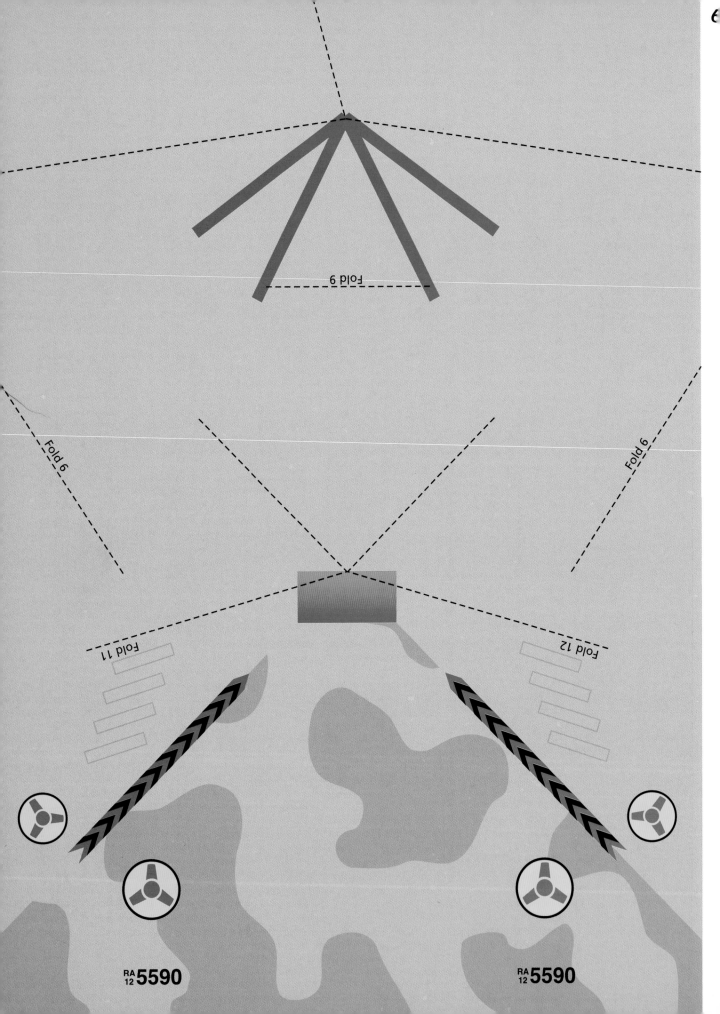

Fold 9

Fold 6

Fold 6

Fold 11

Fold 12

RA 12 5590

RA 12 5590

Origami Plane

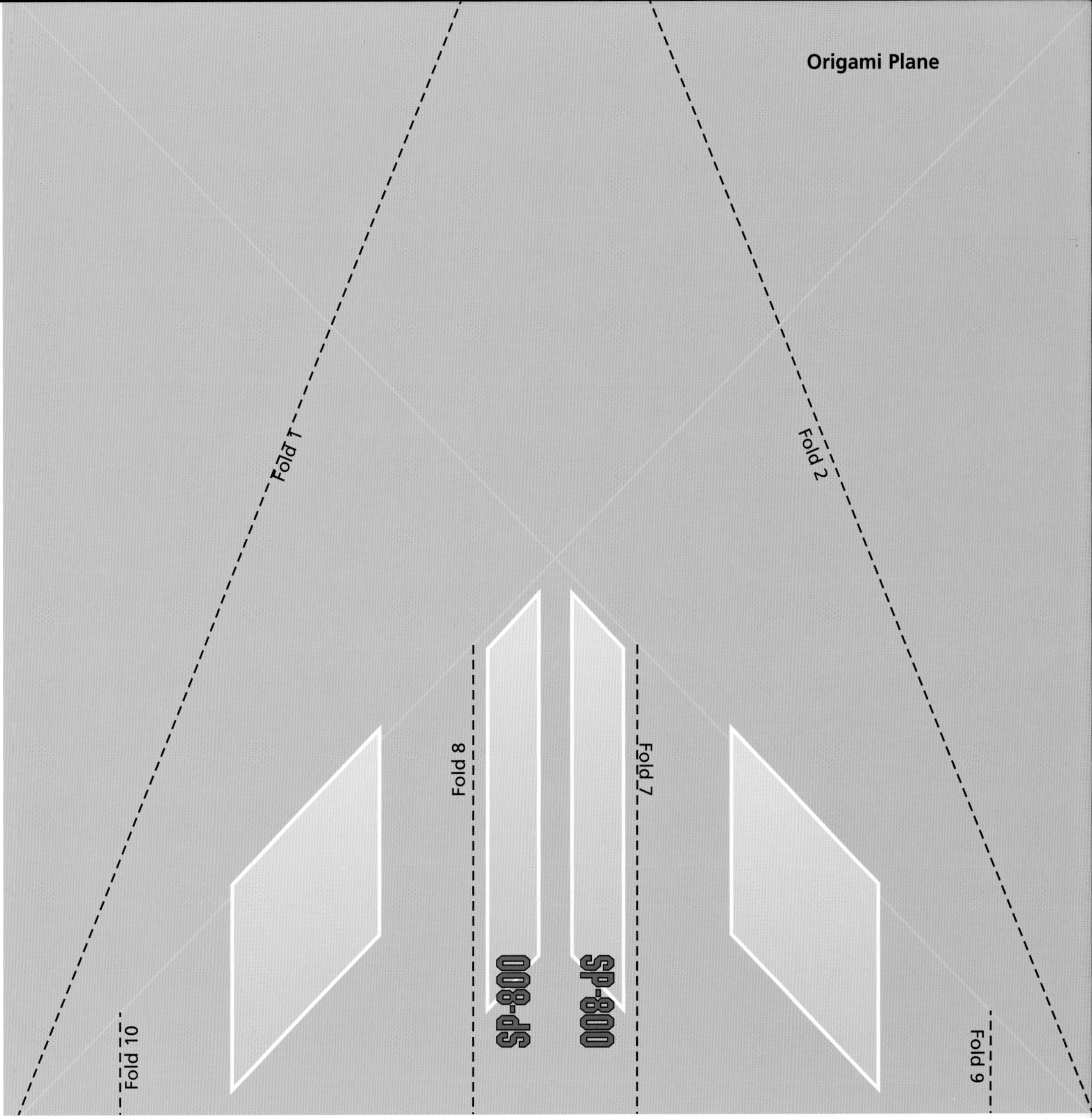

Fold 1

Fold 2

Fold 8

Fold 7

Fold 10

Fold 9

SP-800

SP-800

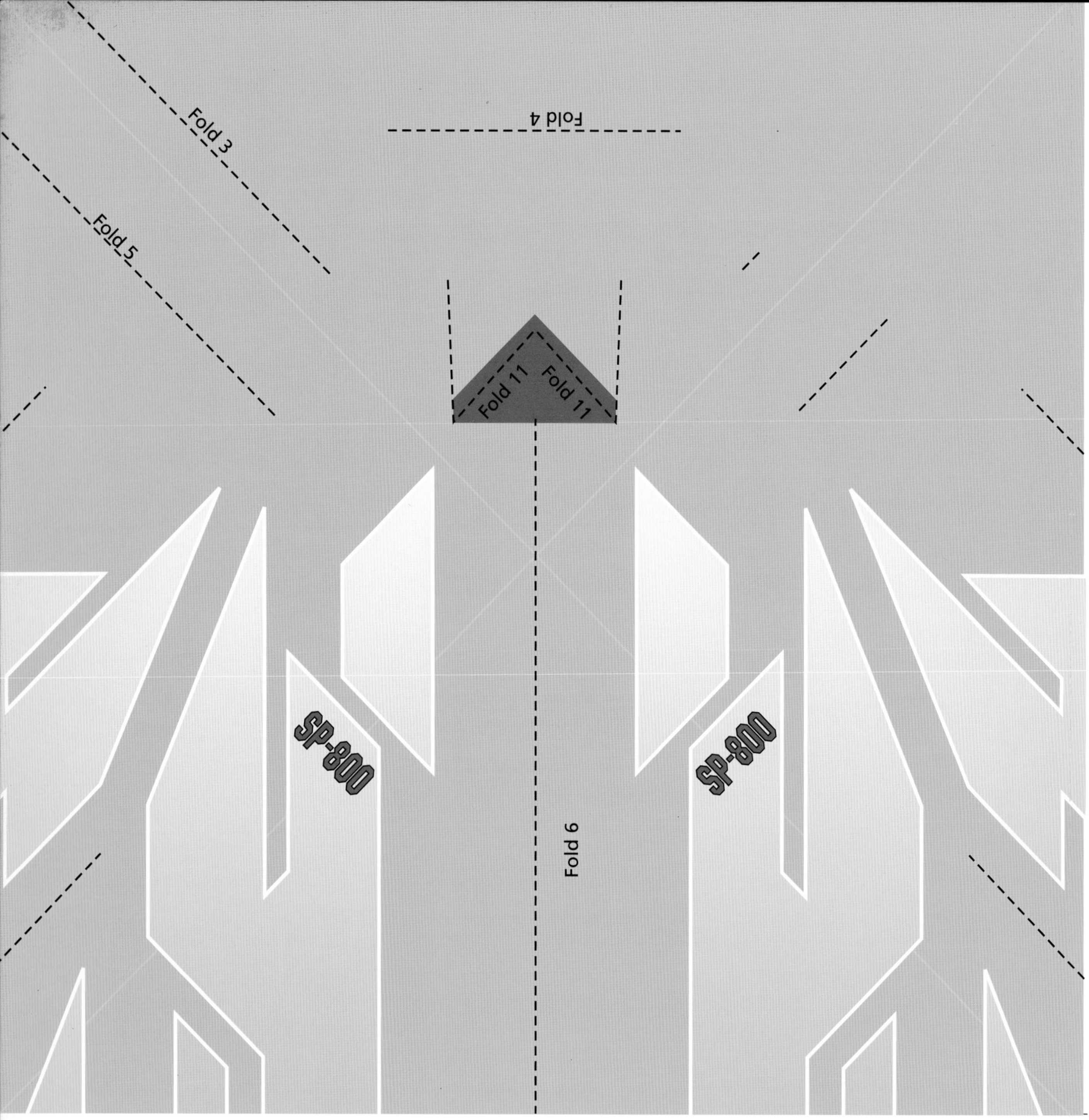

Fold 3

Fold 5

Fold 4

Fold 11   Fold 11

SP-800

SP-800

Fold 6

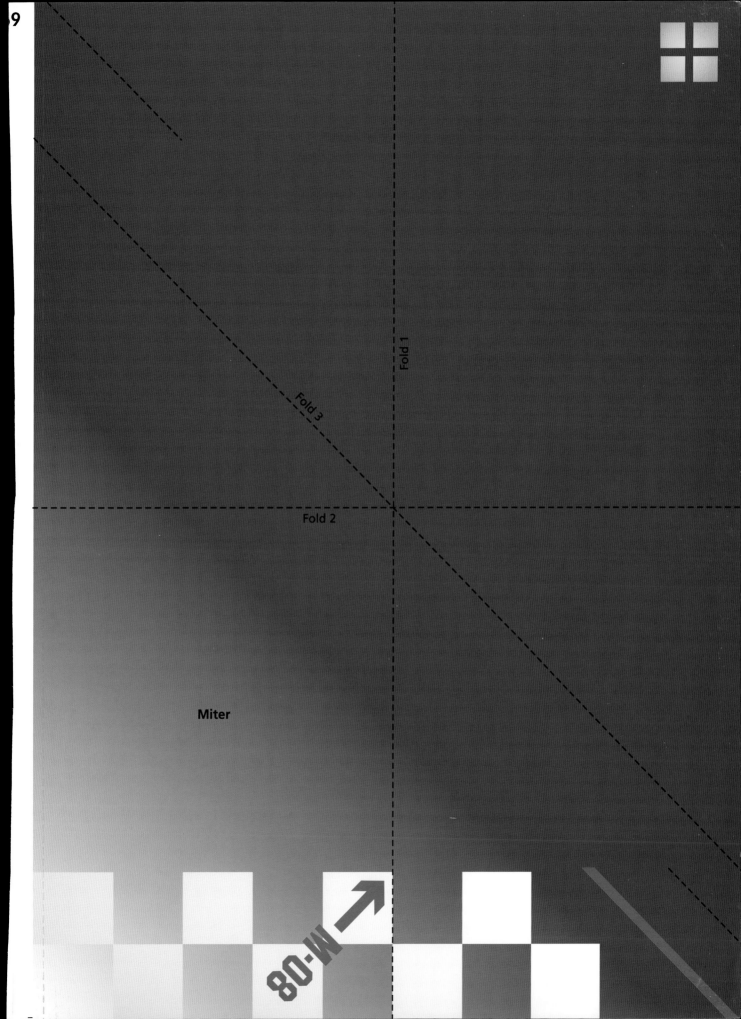

9

Fold 1

Fold 3

Fold 2

Miter

M-08

M-08

Fold 5

Fold 4

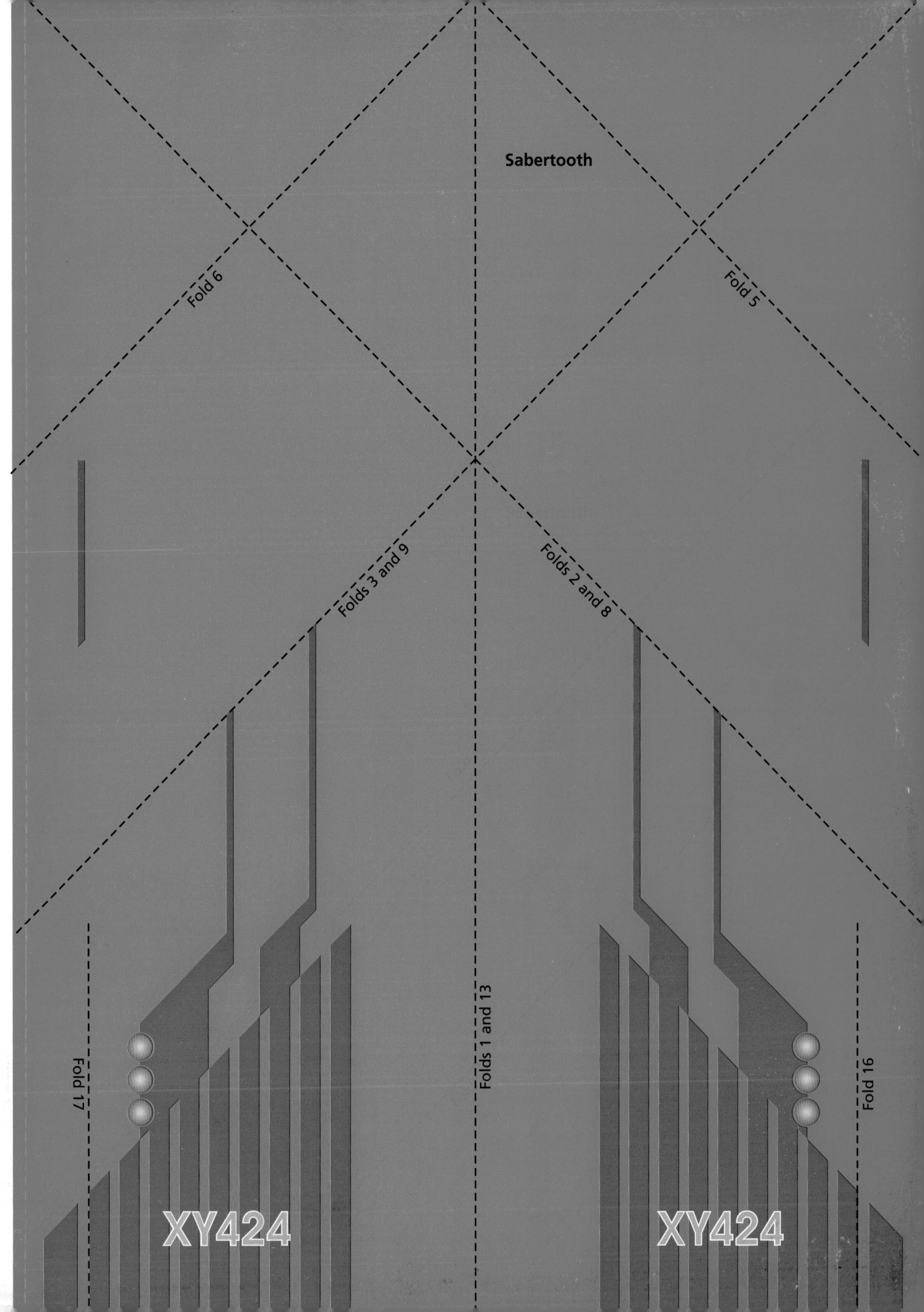

Sabertooth

Fold 6

Fold 5

Folds 3 and 9

Folds 2 and 8

Folds 1 and 13

Fold 17

Fold 16

XY424

XY424

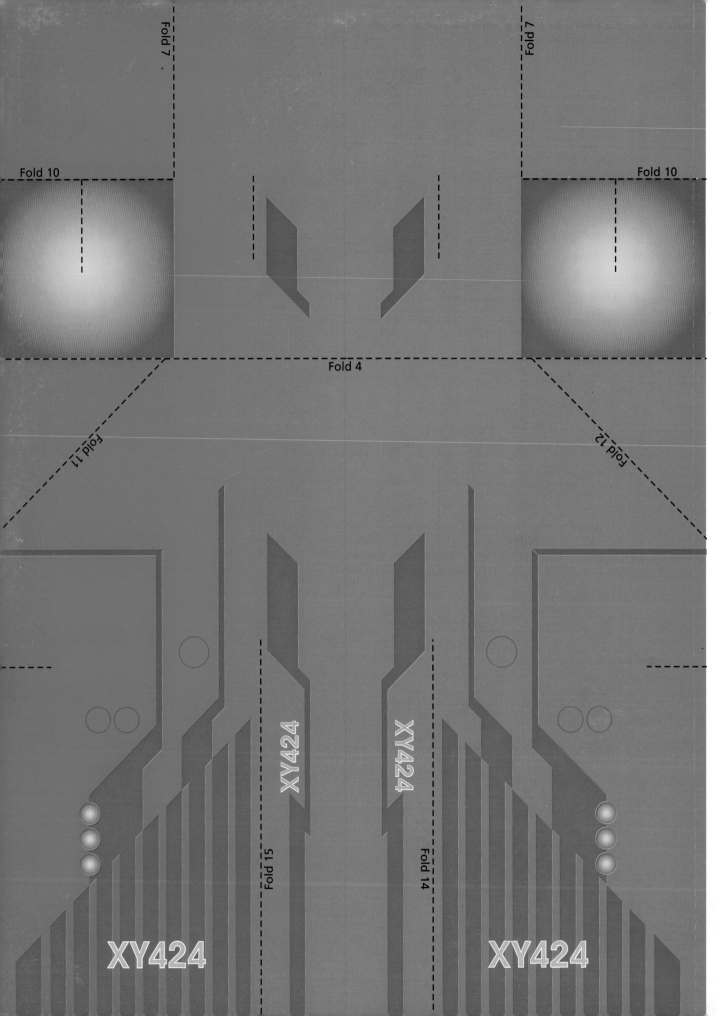